CUDDLE C
COZY CAMPING COLORING BOOK

BERGAMOT PUBLISHING

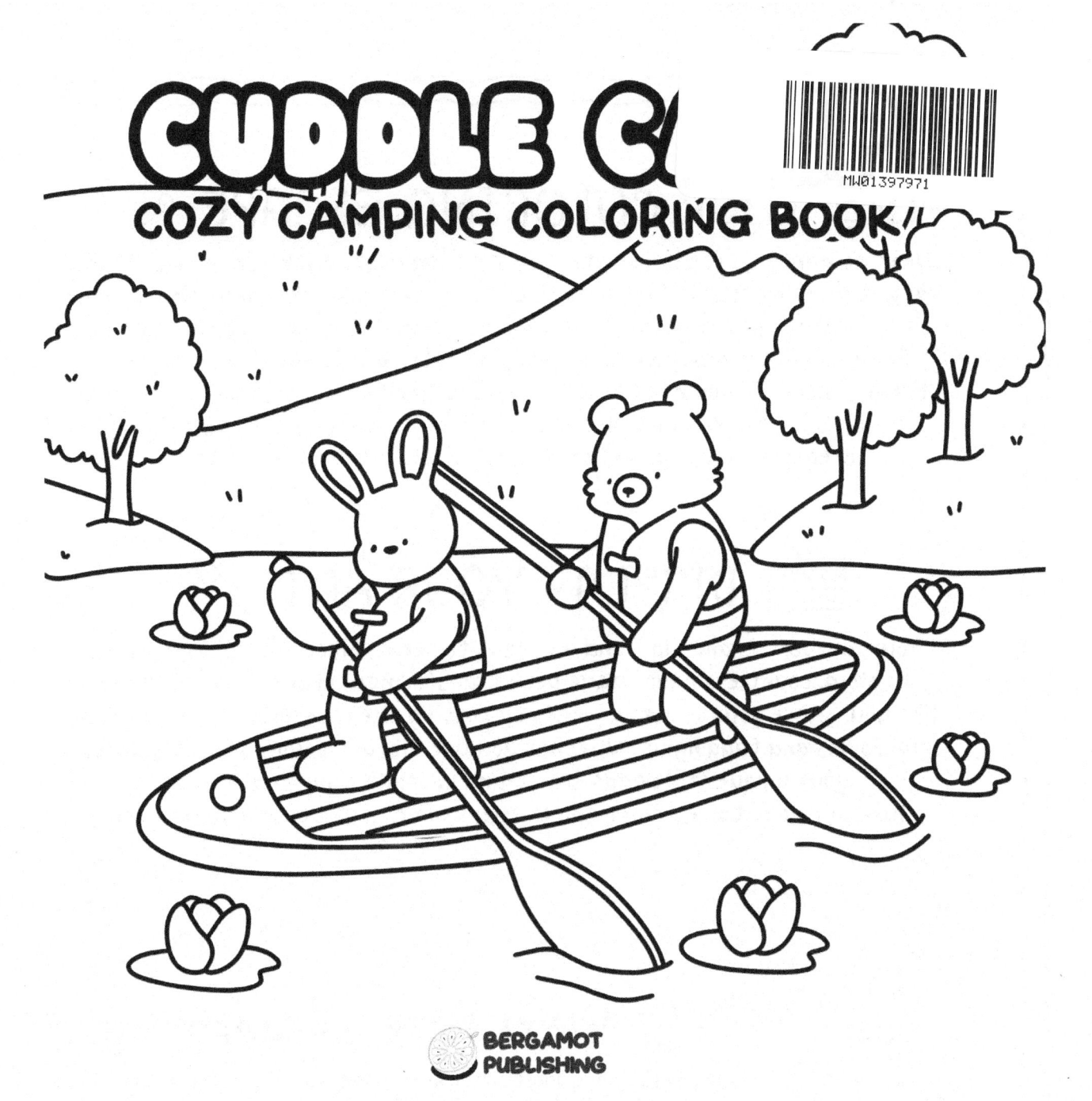

Copyright © 2025 by Bergamot Publishing

All rights reserved. No part of this publication may be reproduced, distributed, or transmitted in any form or by any means, including photocopying, recording, or other electronic or mechanical methods, without the prior written permission of Bergamot Publishing, except in the case of brief quotations used in reviews or promotional materials.

YOUR COLORING ESCAPE

We're so happy you're here with this coloring book. With school, work, and daily responsibilities, it's important to take some time for yourself. Coloring is a great way to relax and be creative, helping you forget your worries. Each picture is designed to inspire and calm you, giving you a peaceful break whenever you need it. Whether you like bright, bold colors or soft, gentle ones, there's no right or wrong way to color these pages. Enjoy creating, relaxing, and finding joy with every colored stroke.

DISPLAY YOUR ART

Your artwork is amazing, and we want to see it! Since our coloring books launched, countless pages have been transformed by creative individuals like you. Share your finished pieces by posting them on your favorite social platforms and tagging us. Whether you use vibrant colors or soft shades, your unique style adds something special to our community.
Show off your talent and inspire others with your beautiful creations!

We're here to support you!

If you have any questions or need assistance, please reach out to us at info@bergamotpublishing.com. We'd love to hear from you!

SHARE YOUR WONDERFUL ARTWORK WITH US. JOIN OUR COMMUNITY.

@bergamotcoloring

GET 50+ FREE Coloring Pages!

Love what you're coloring?
There's so much more waiting for you!

Scan the QR code below to unlock over
50 extra coloring pages.
Explore new designs, spark your
creativity, and keep the fun going.
Happy coloring!

THIS BOOK BELONGS TO

_____
_____

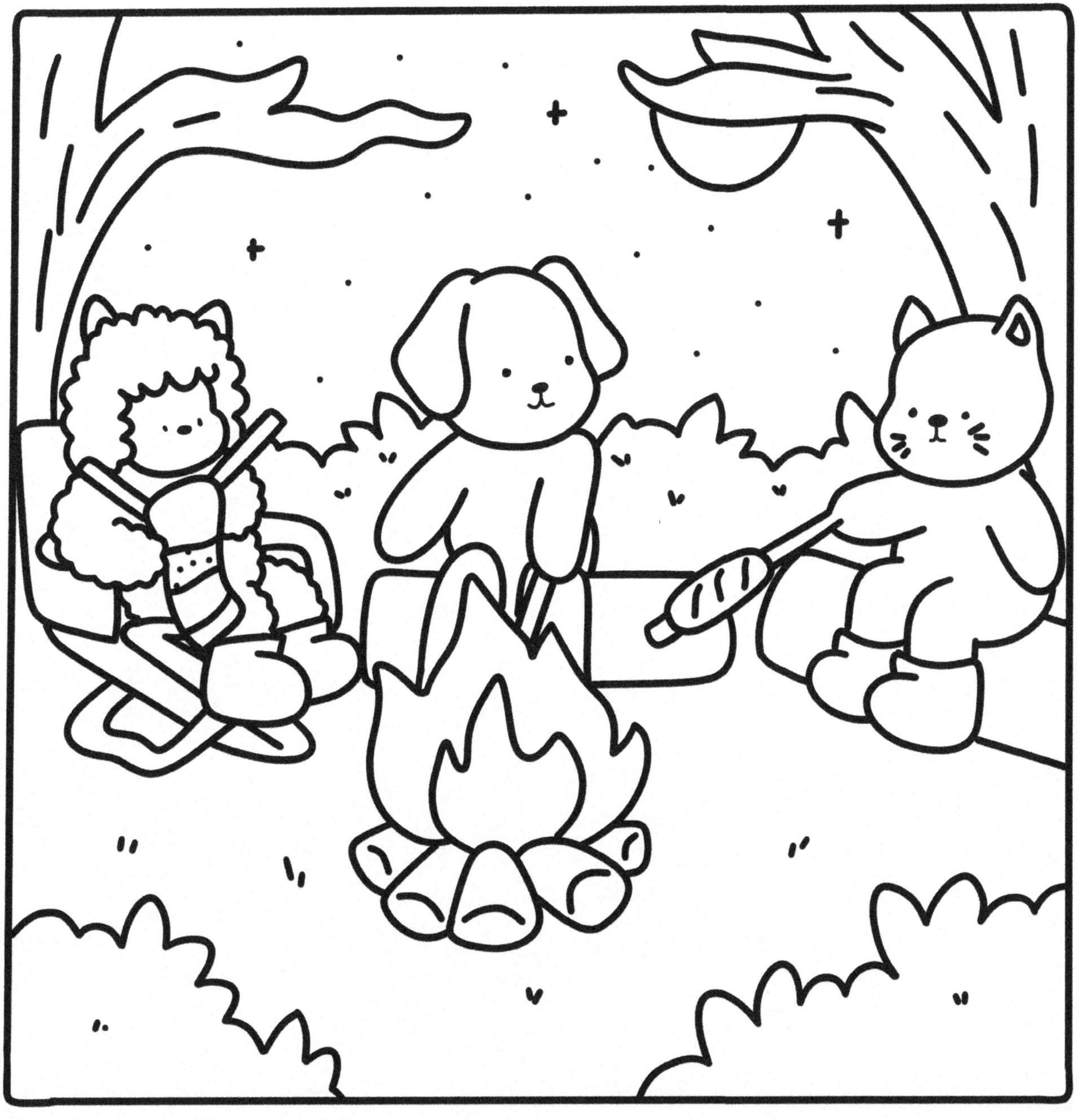

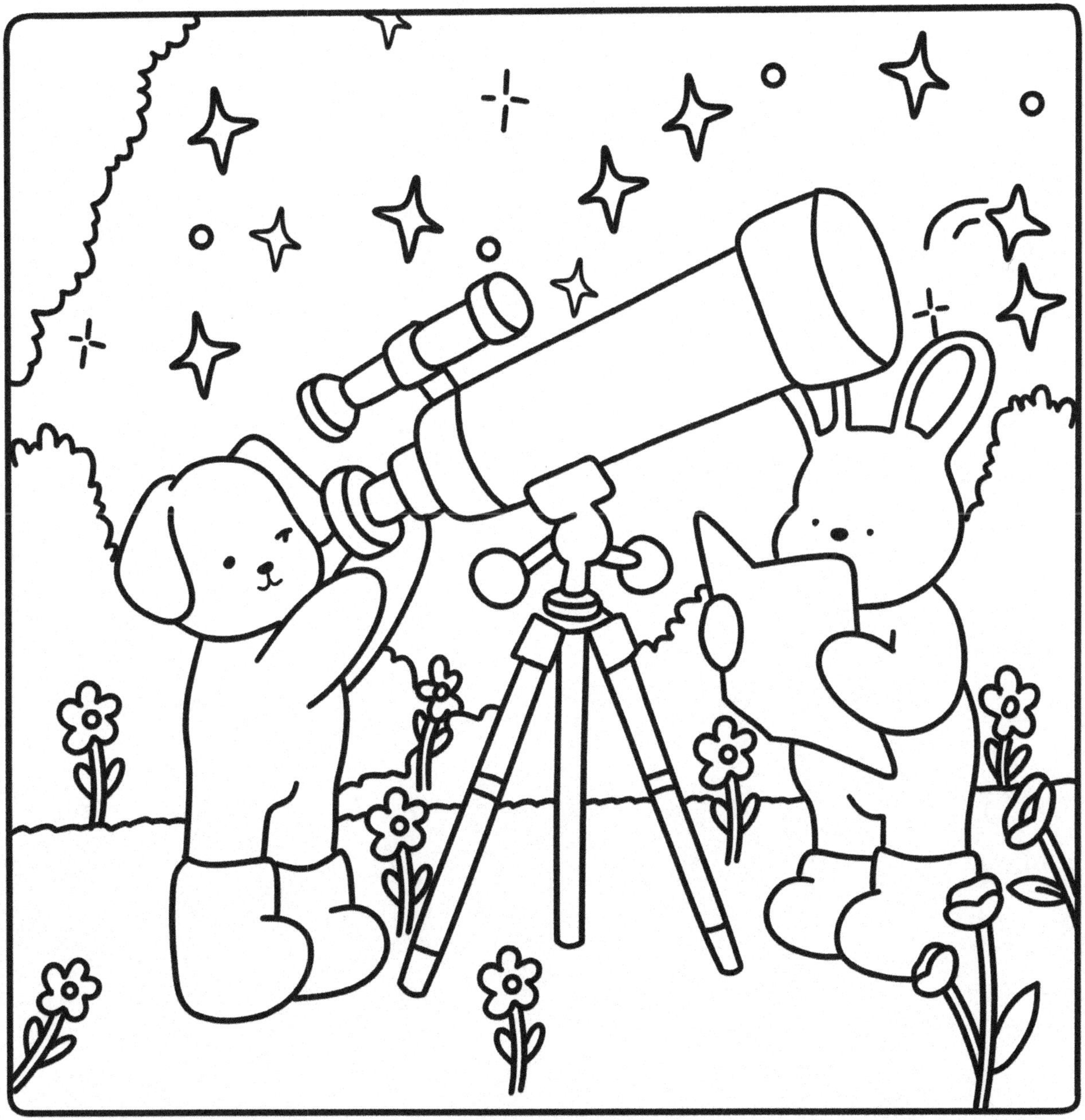

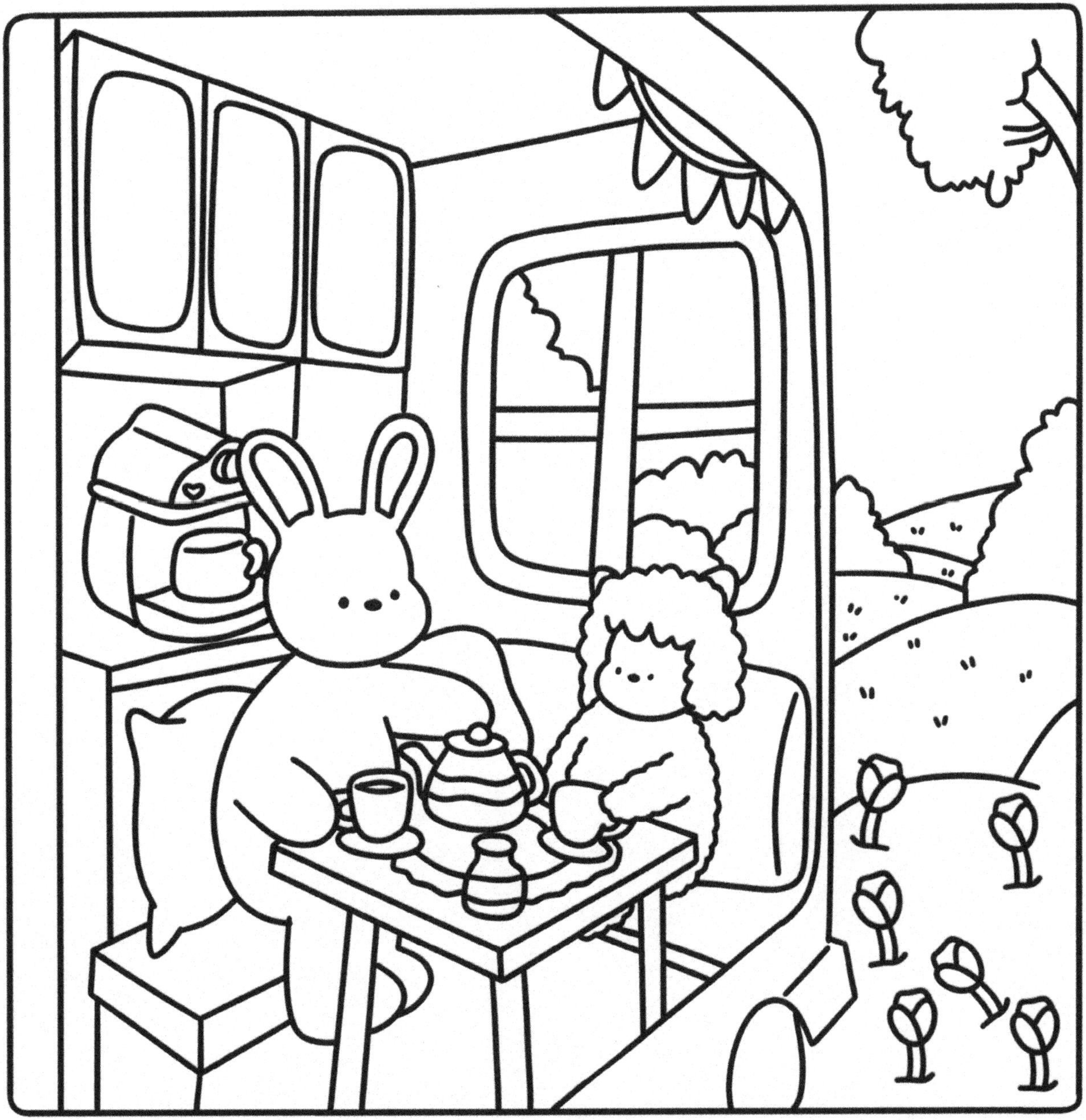

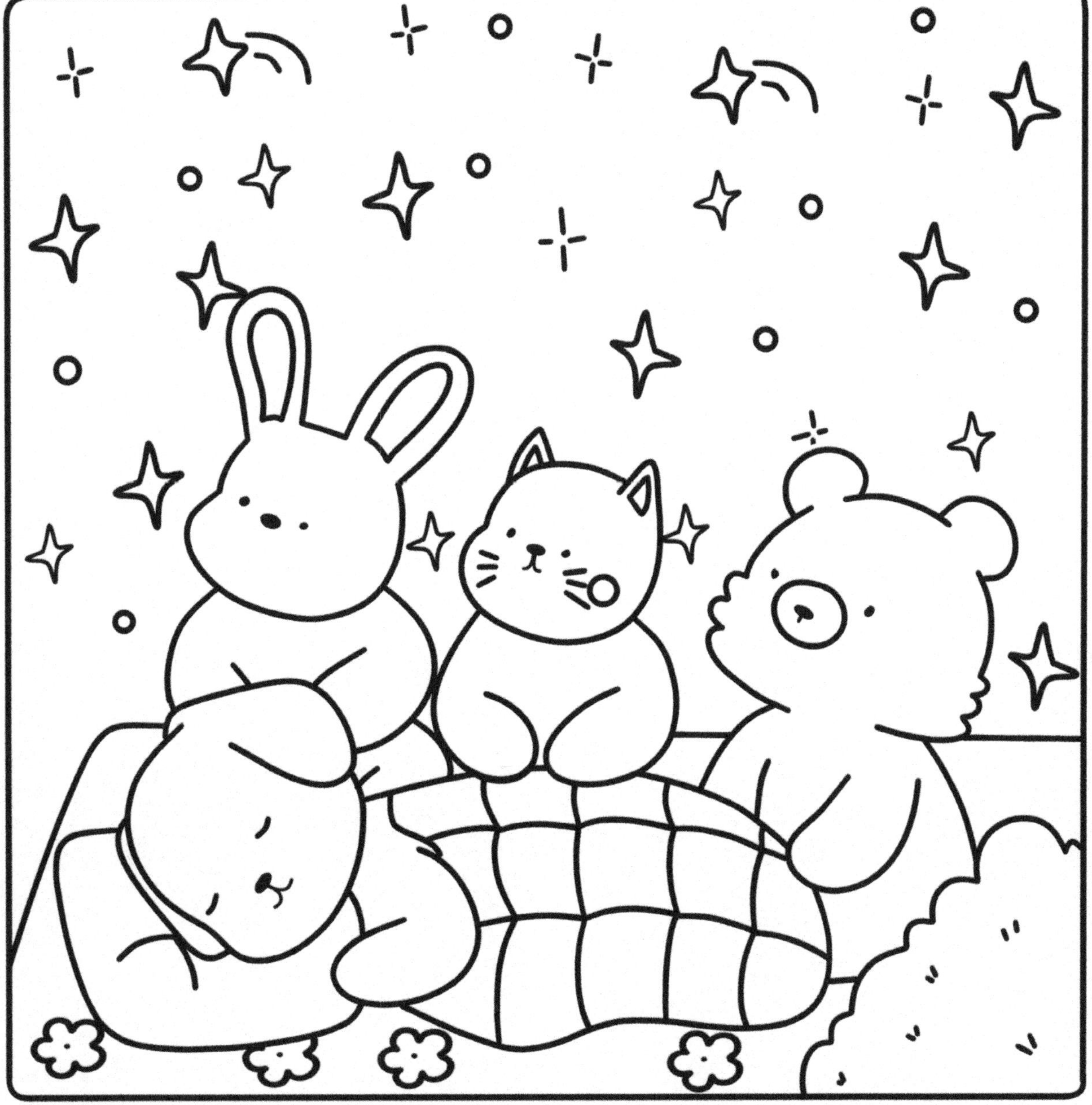

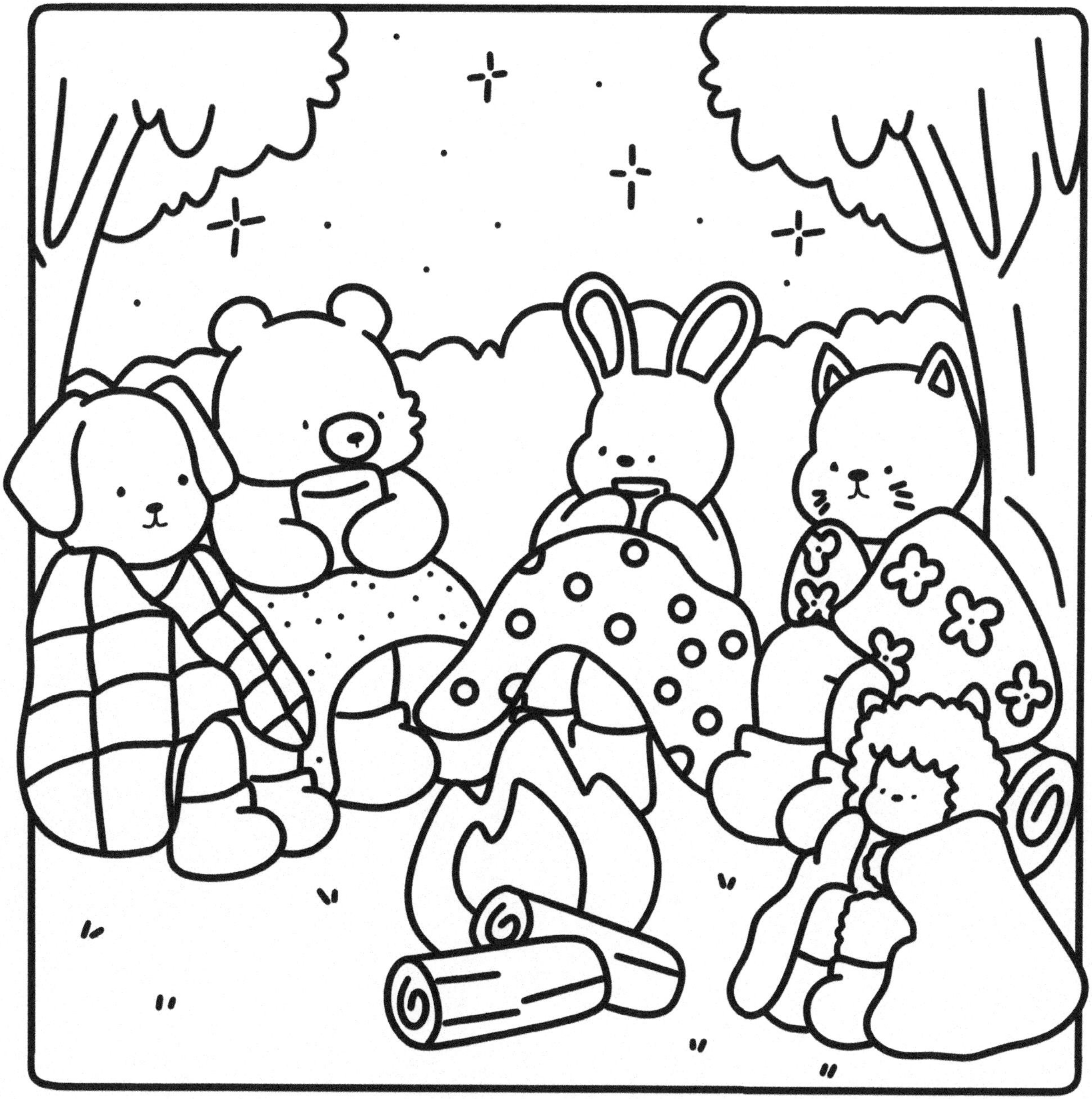

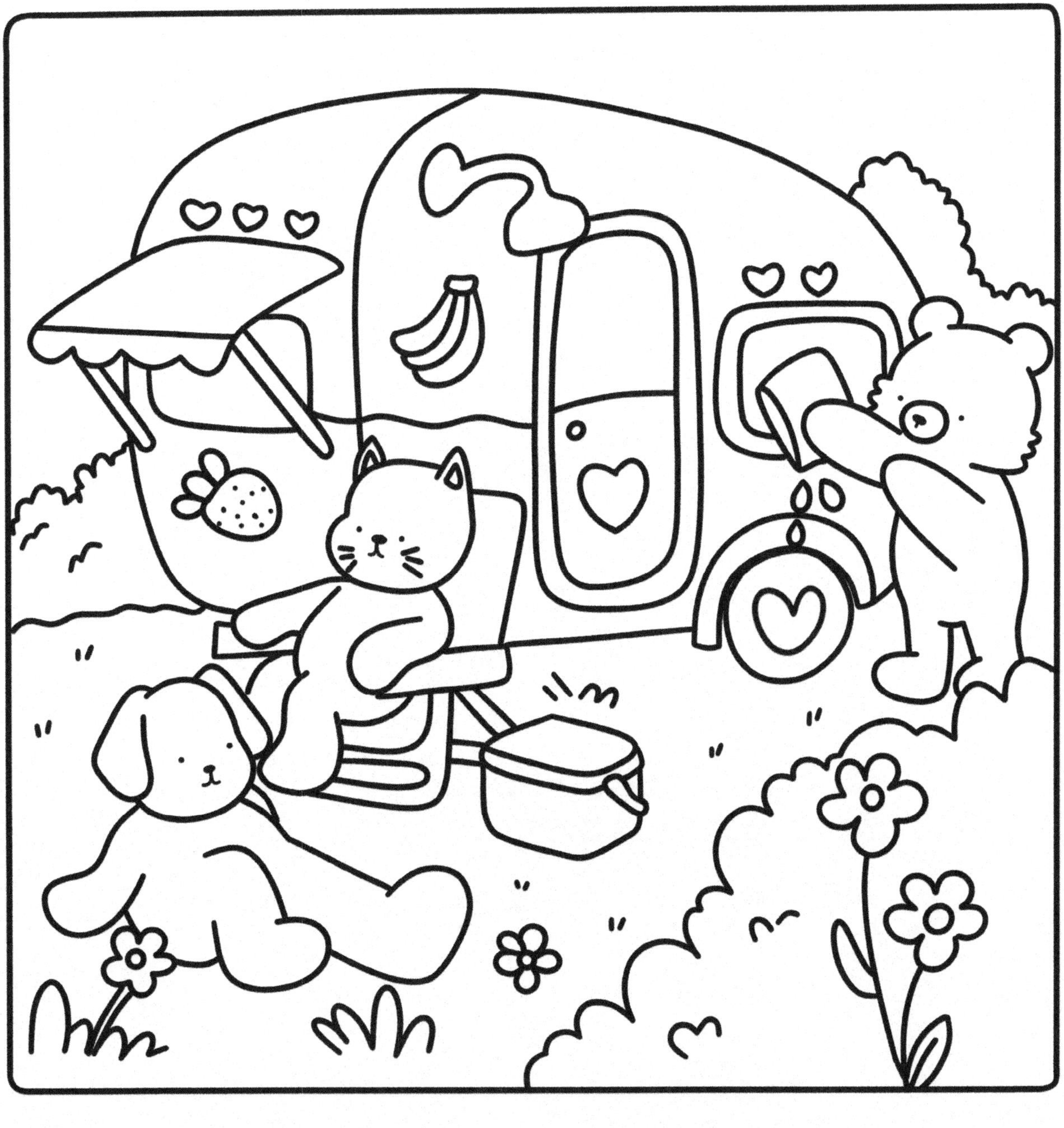

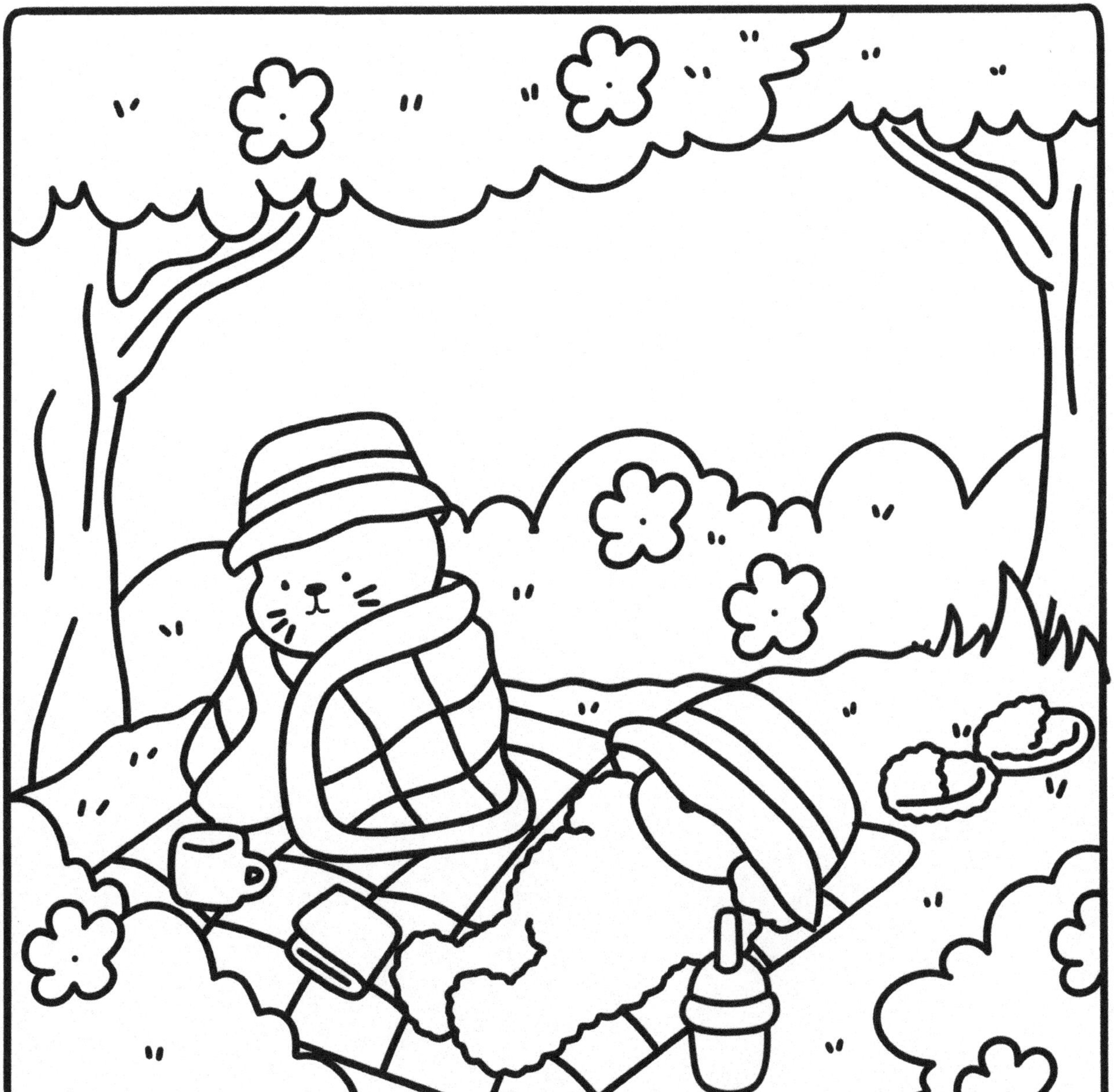

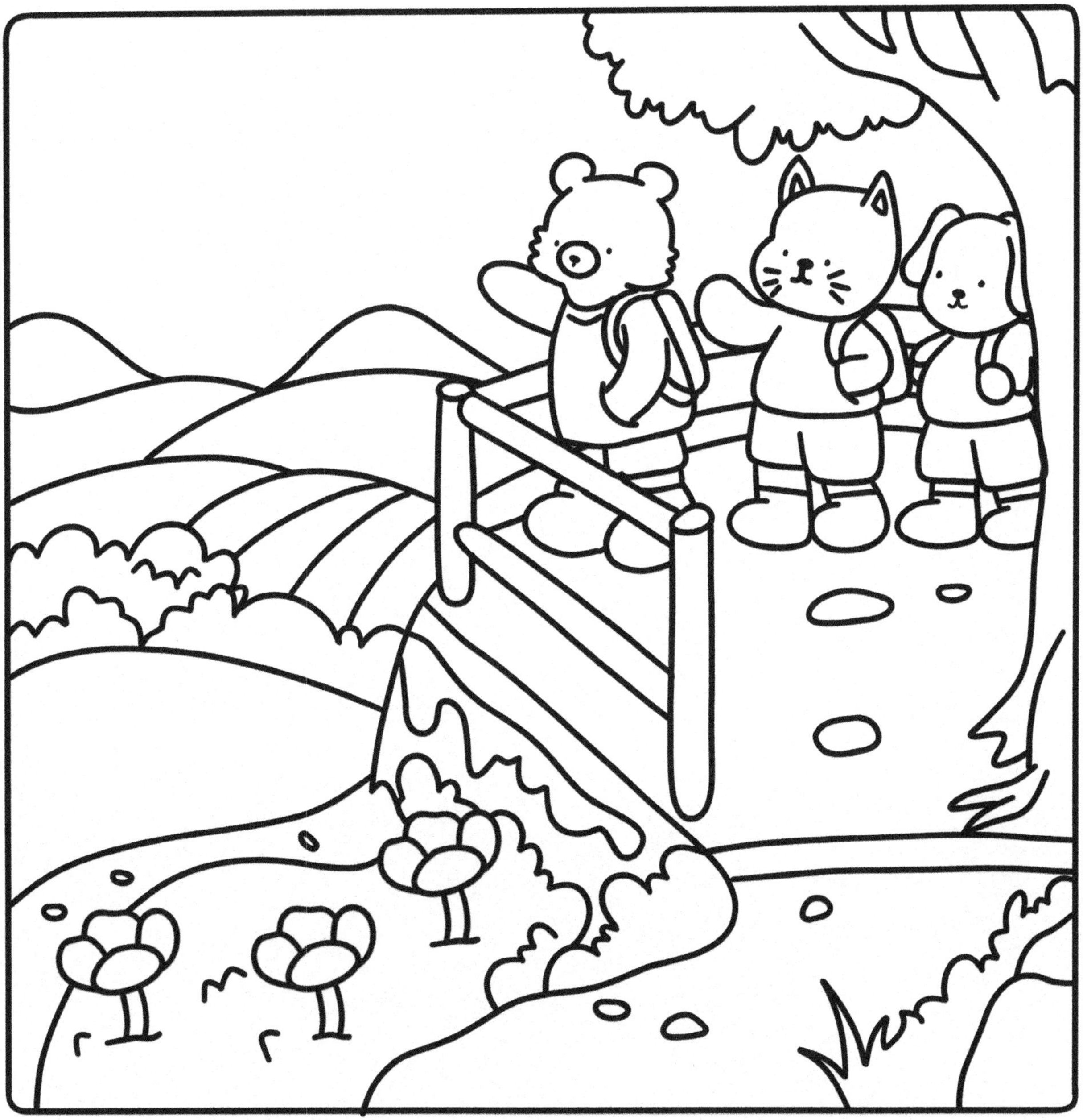

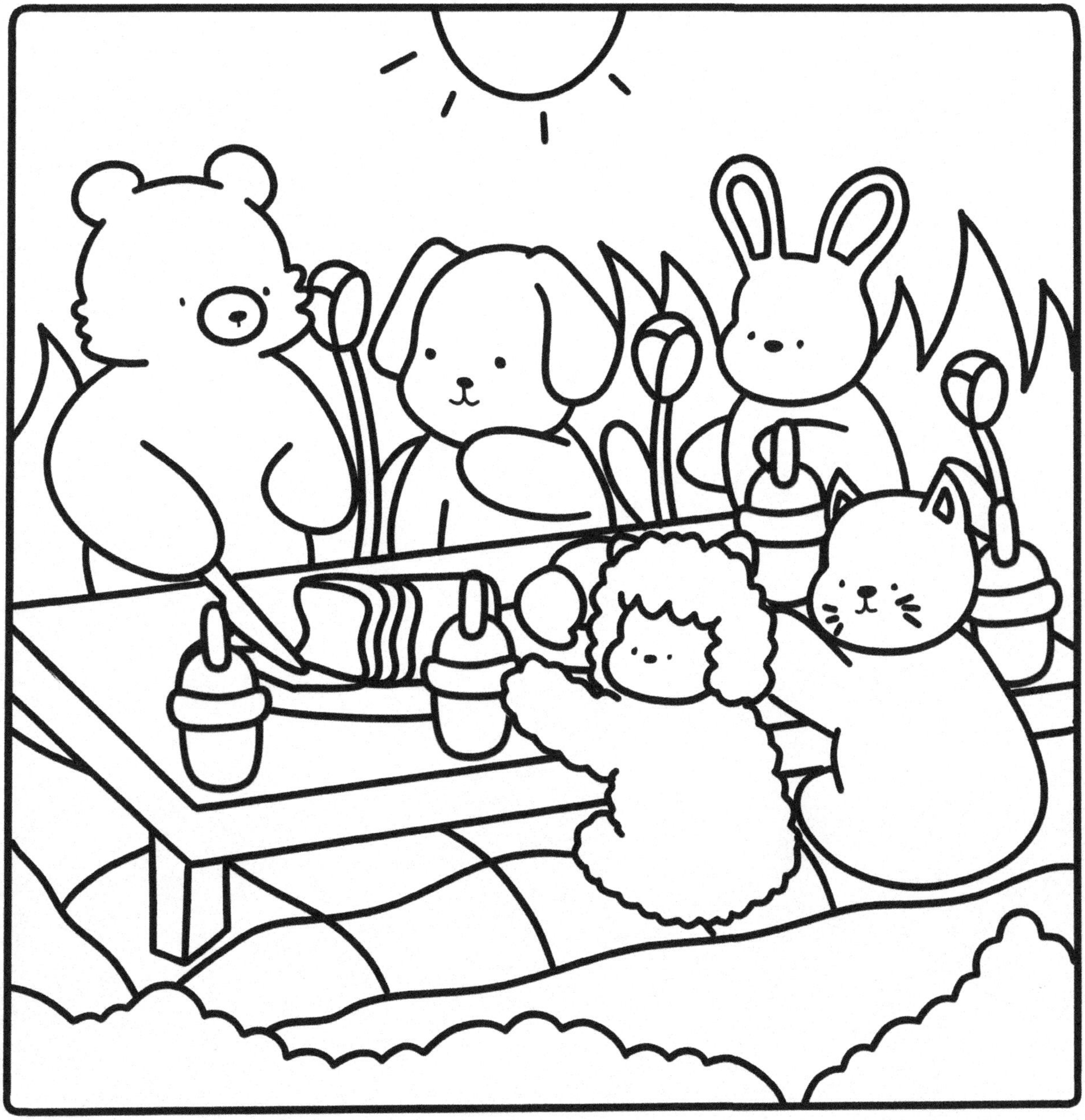

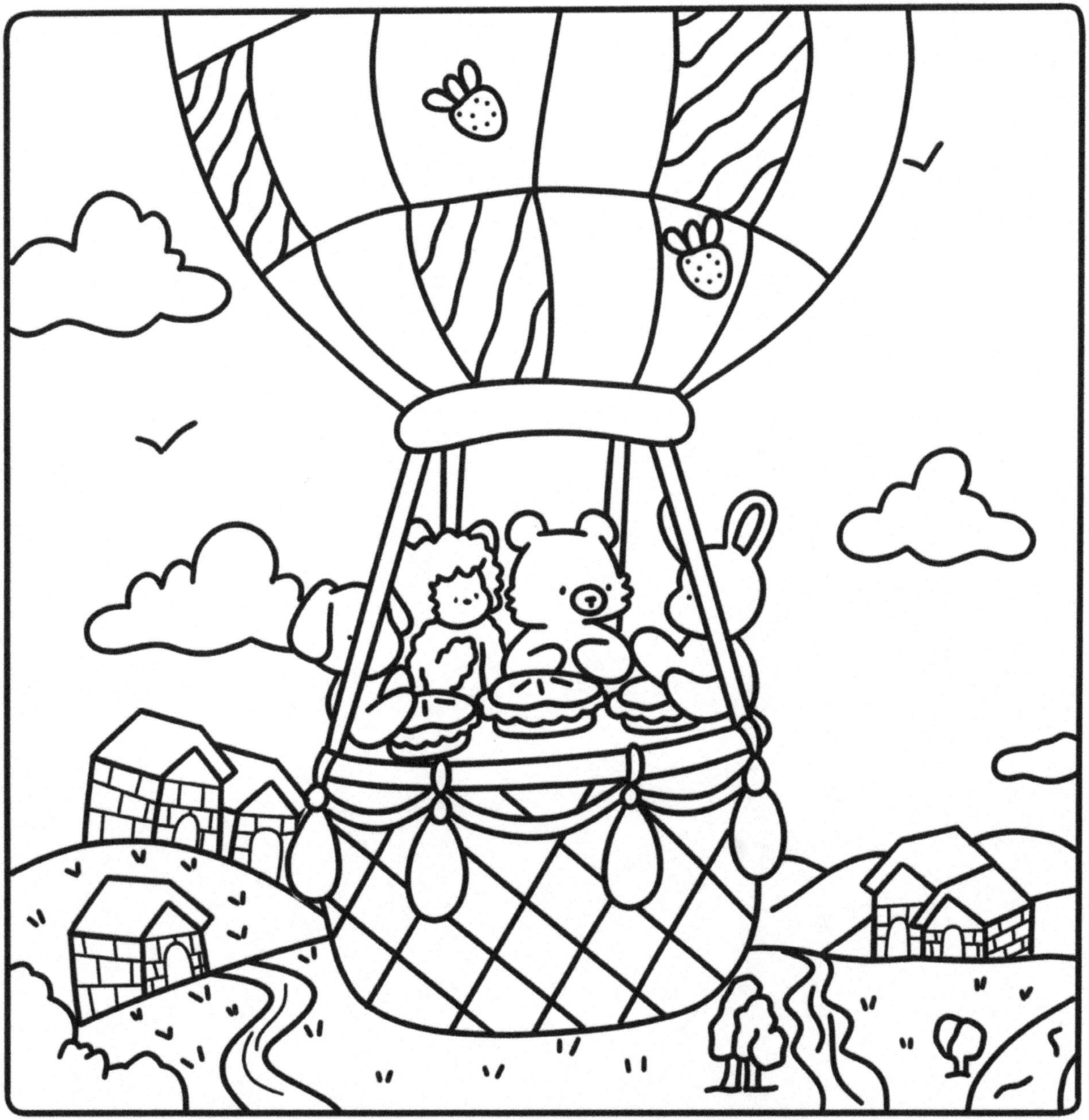

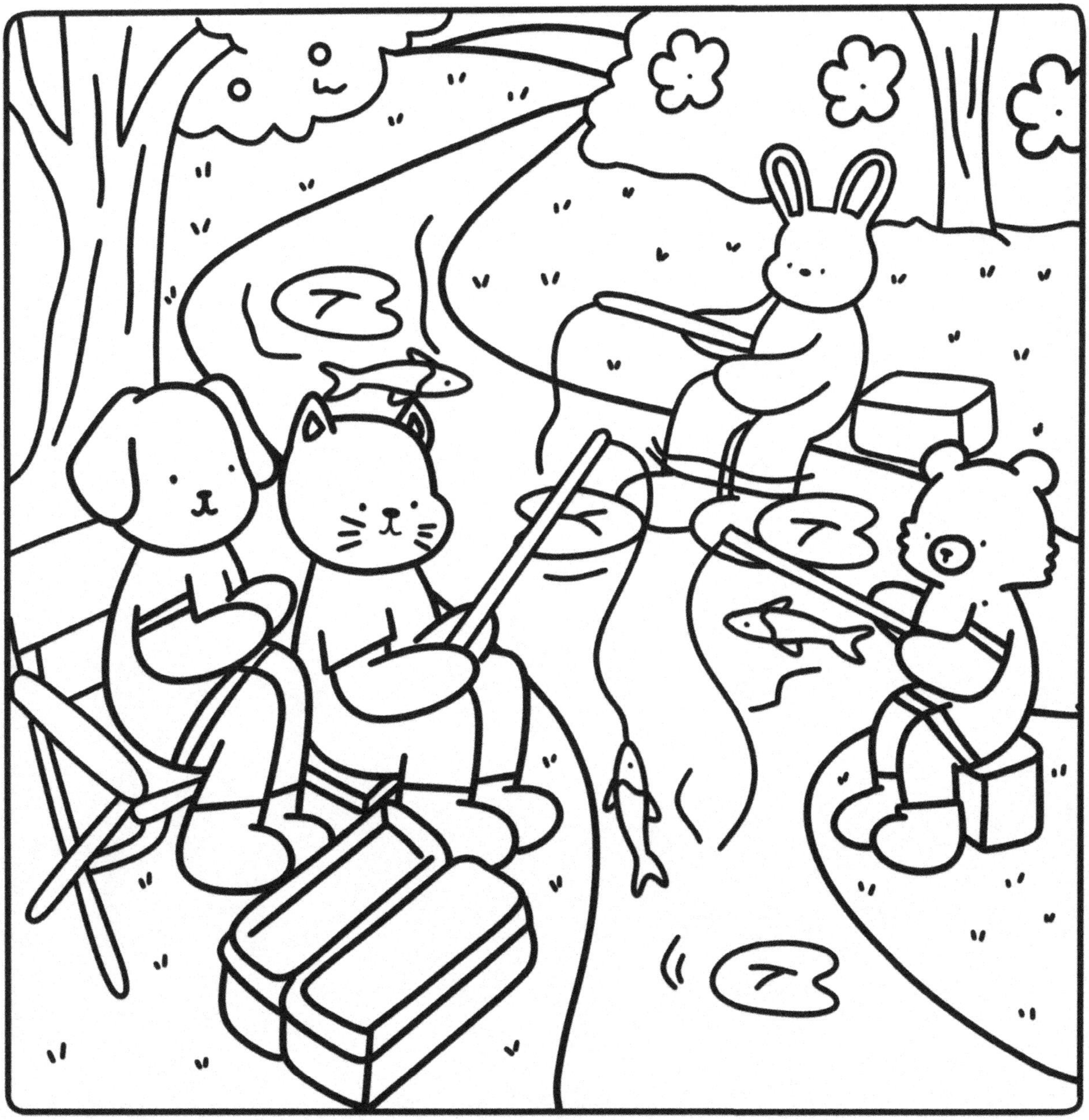

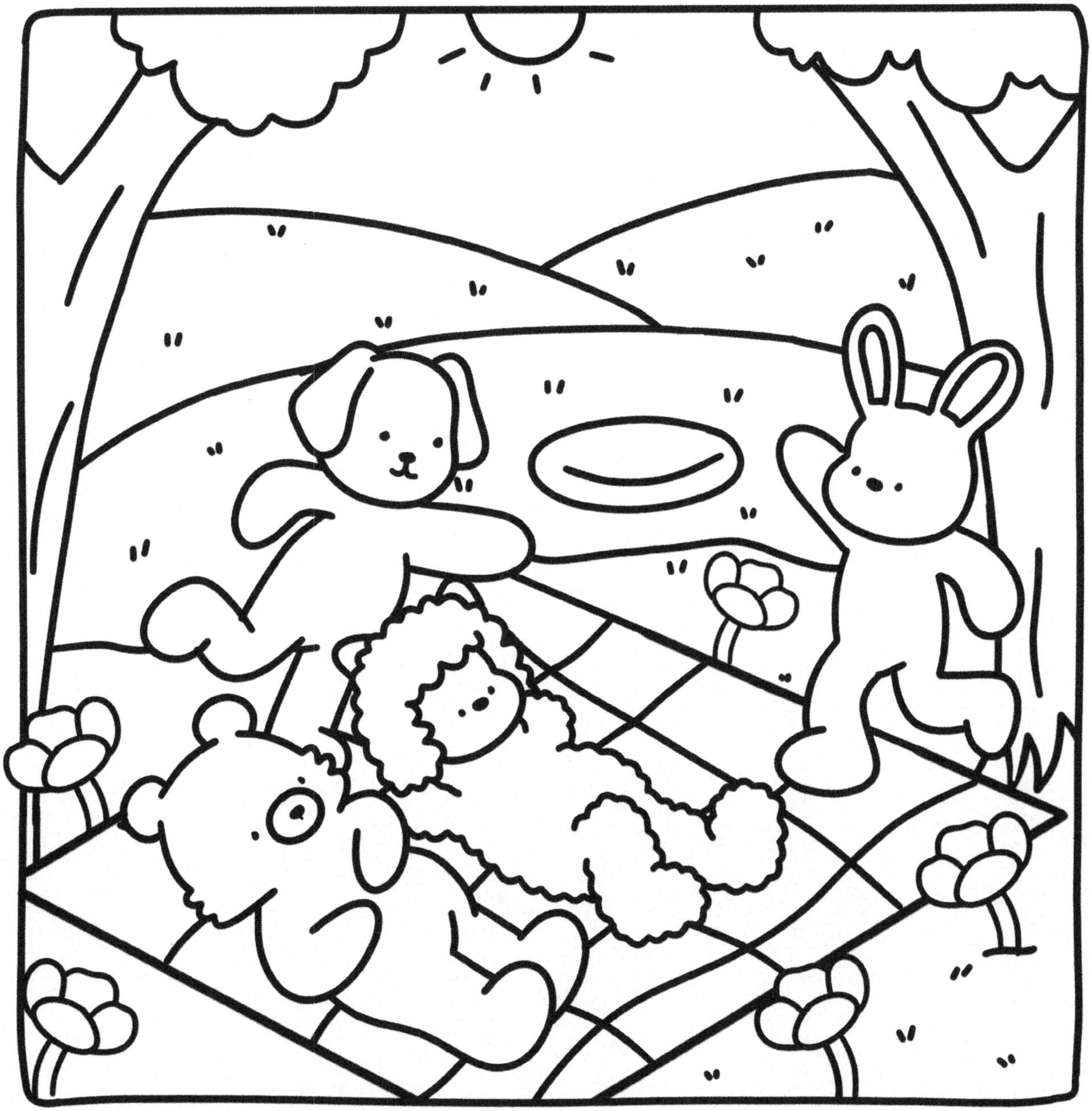

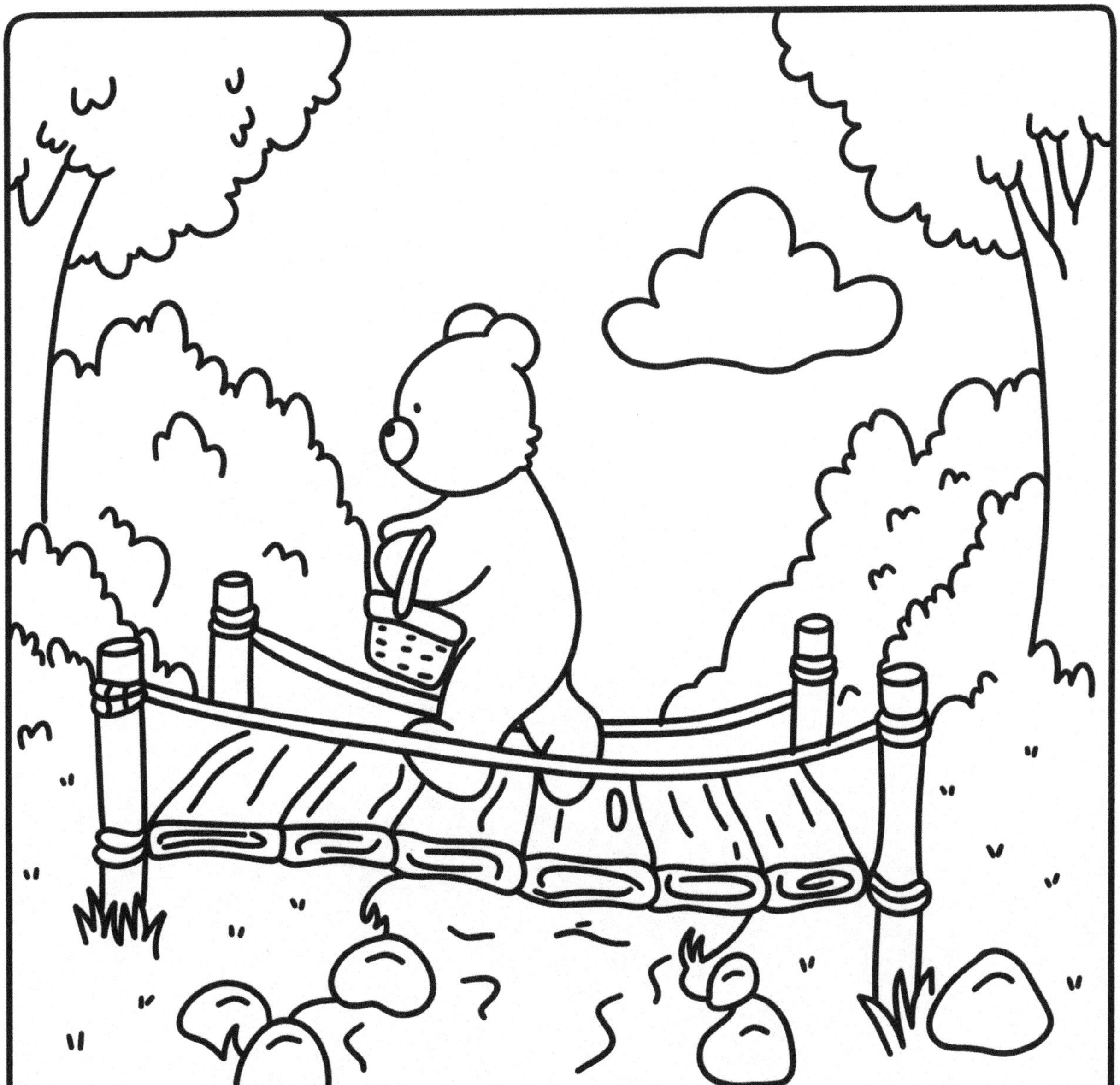

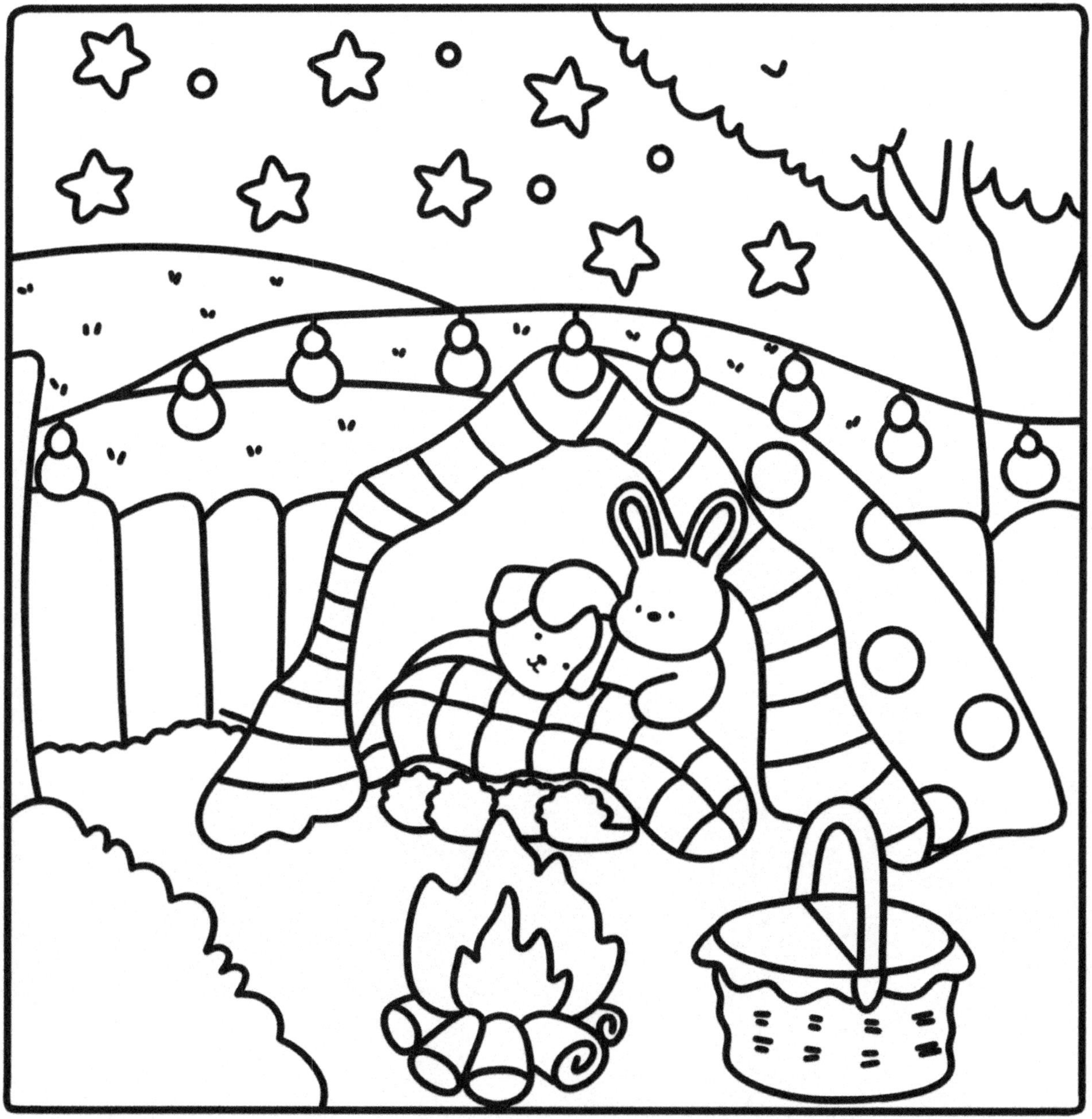

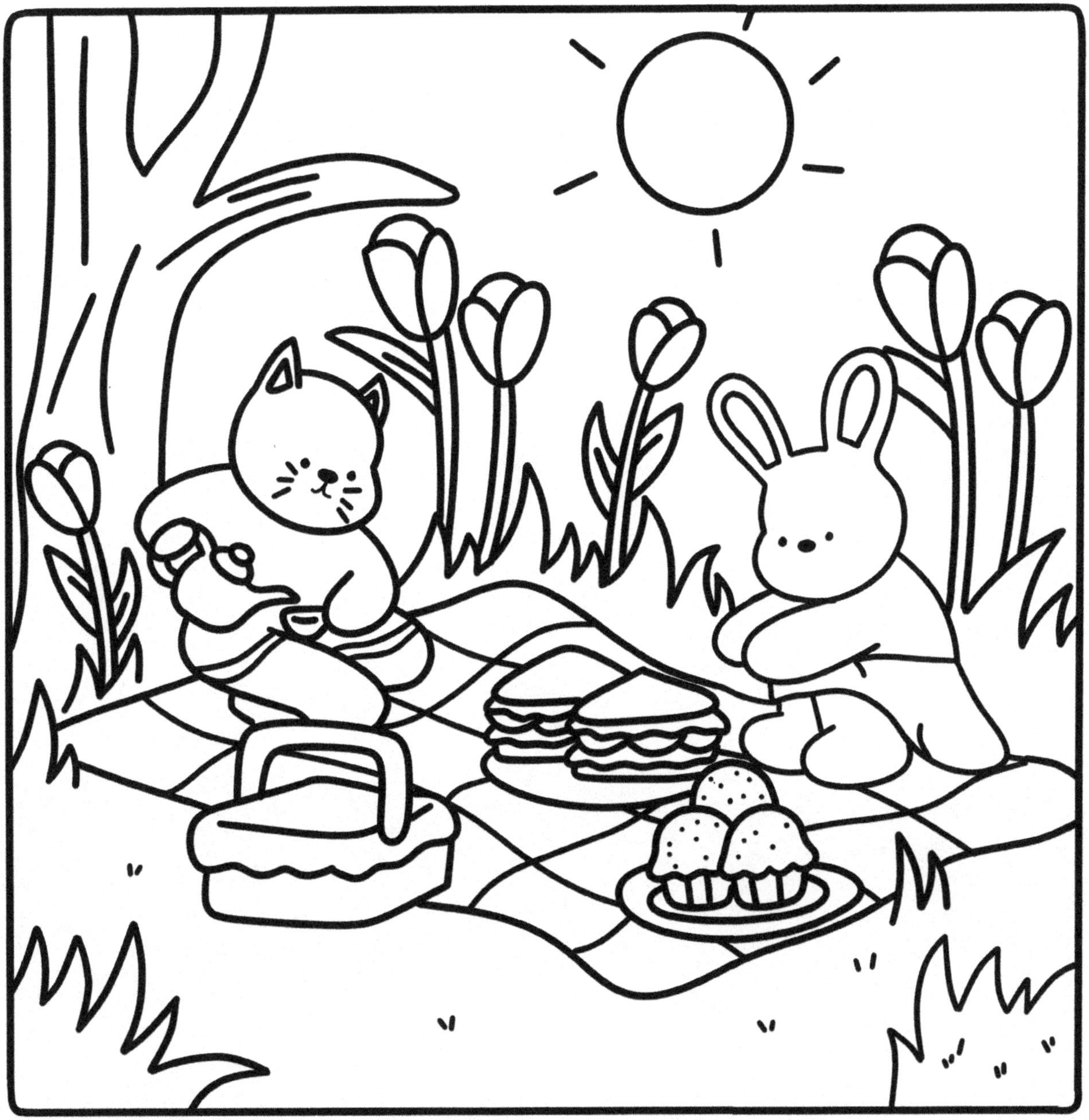

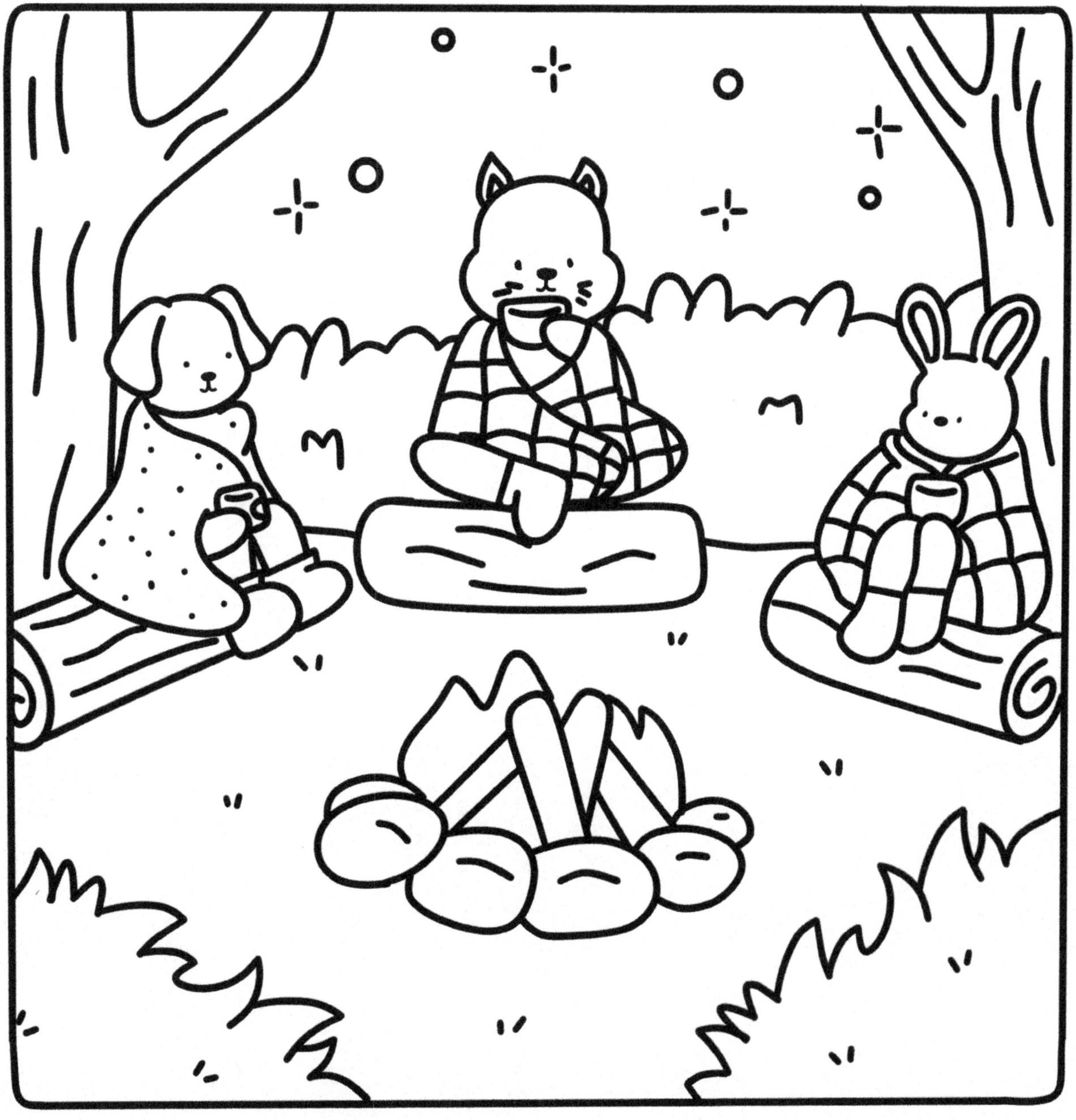

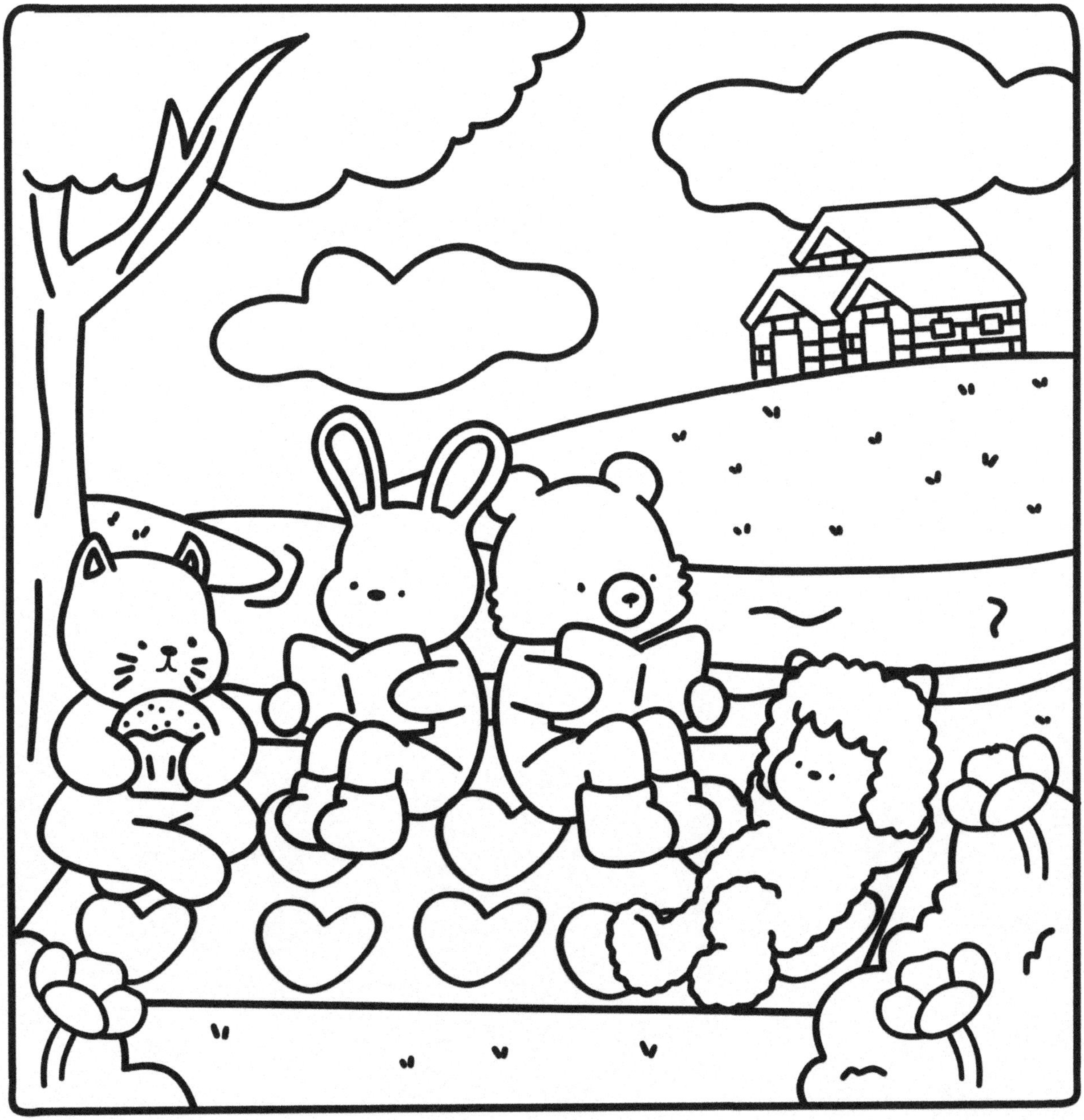

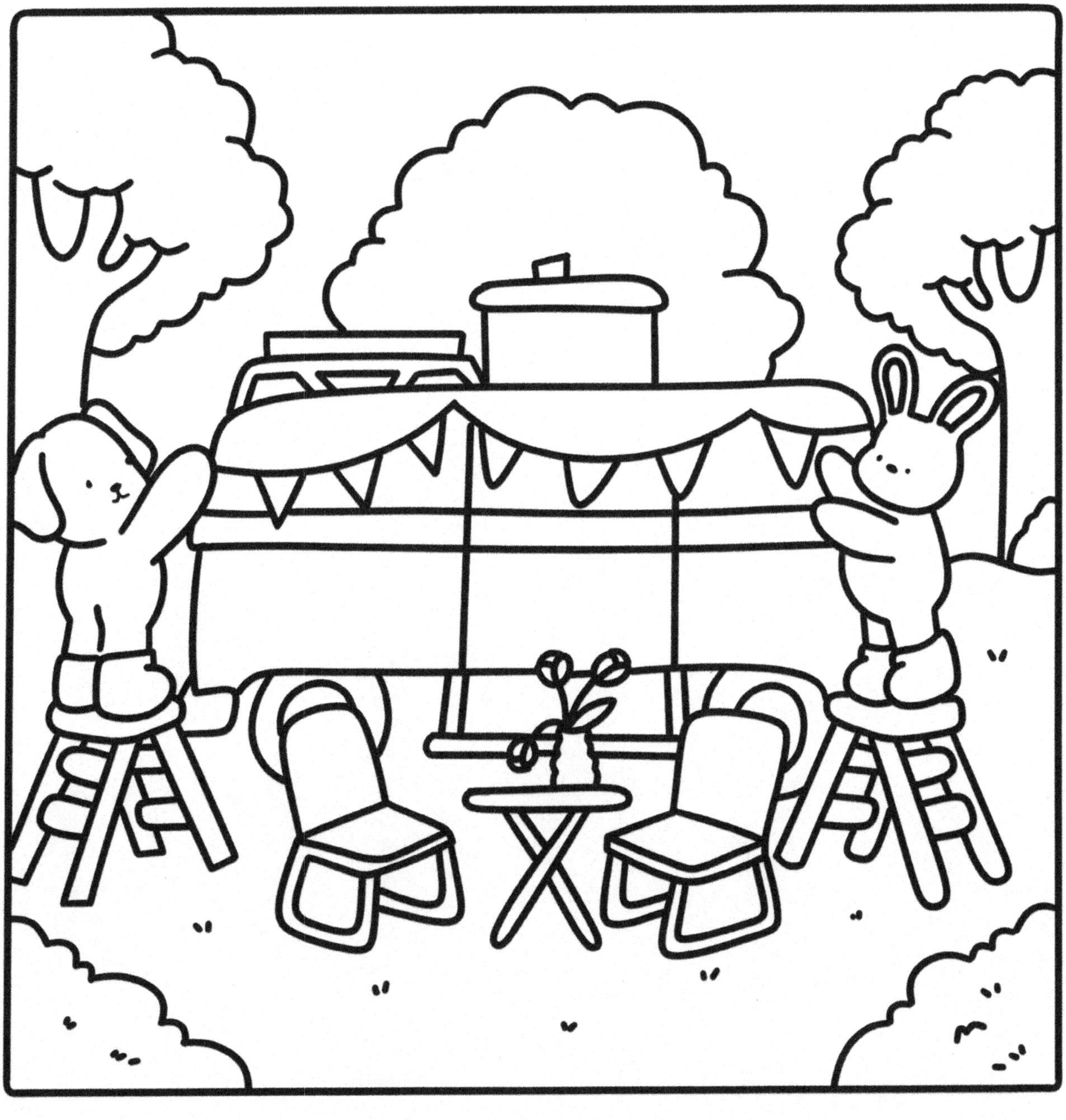

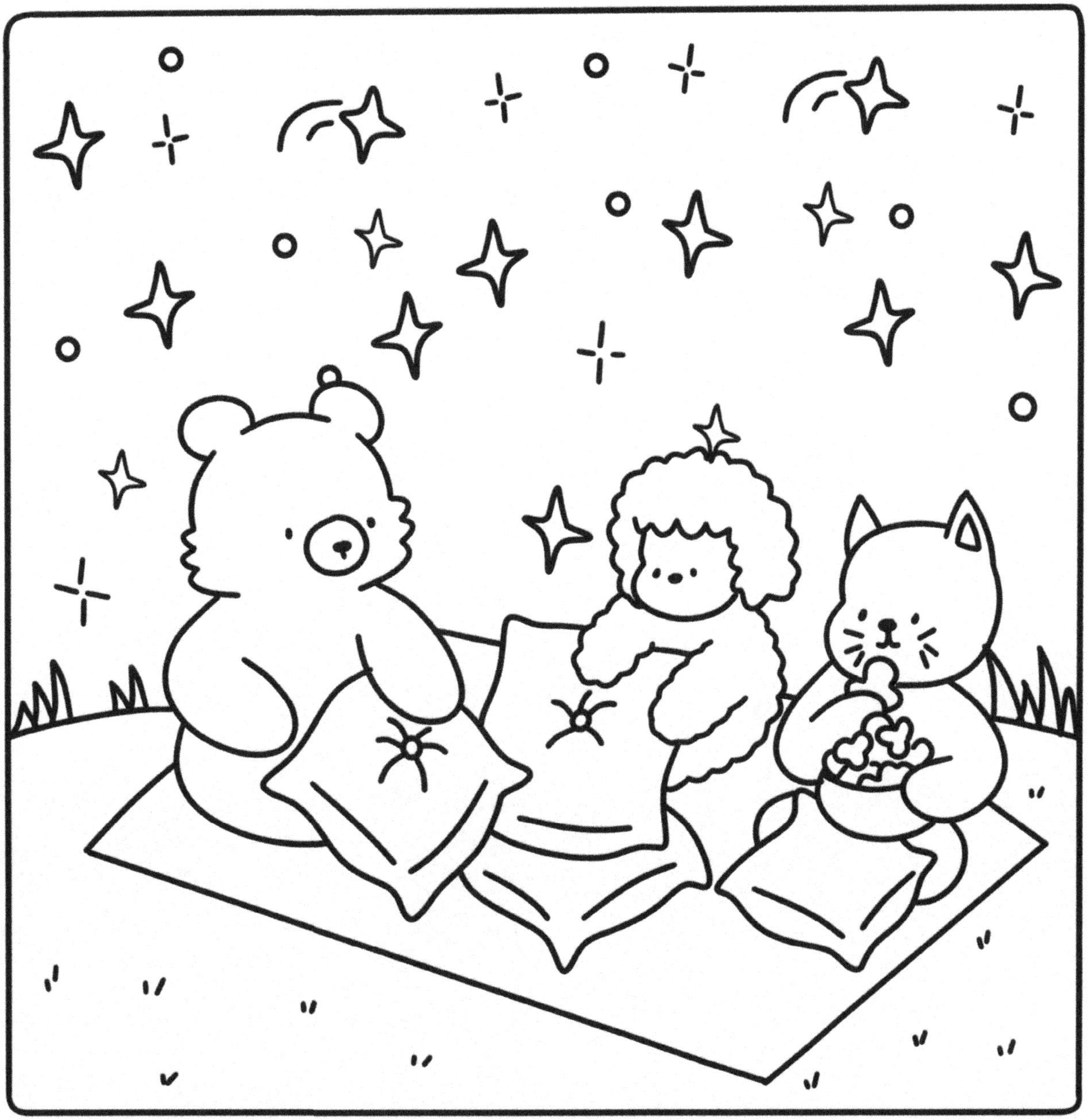

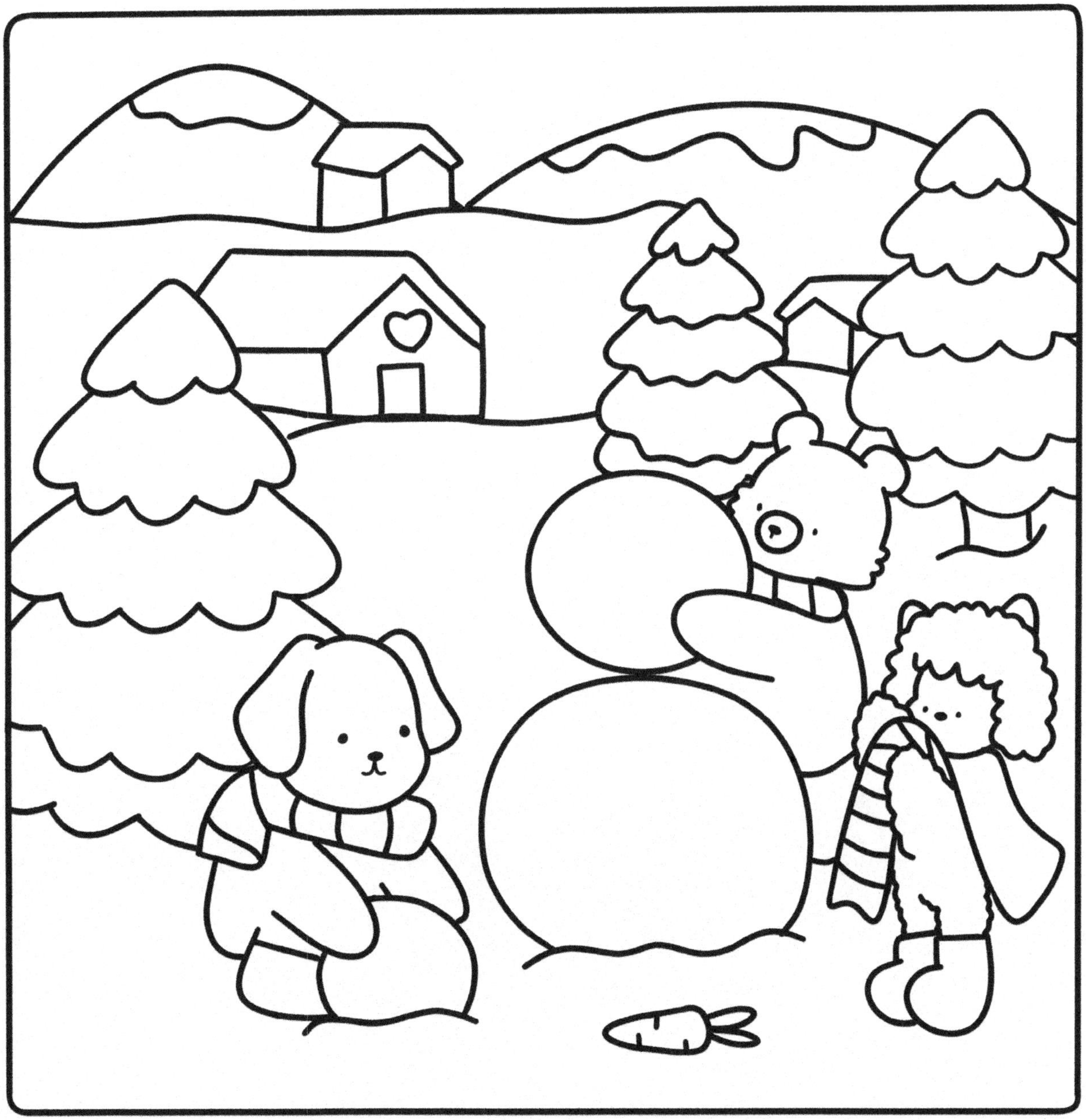

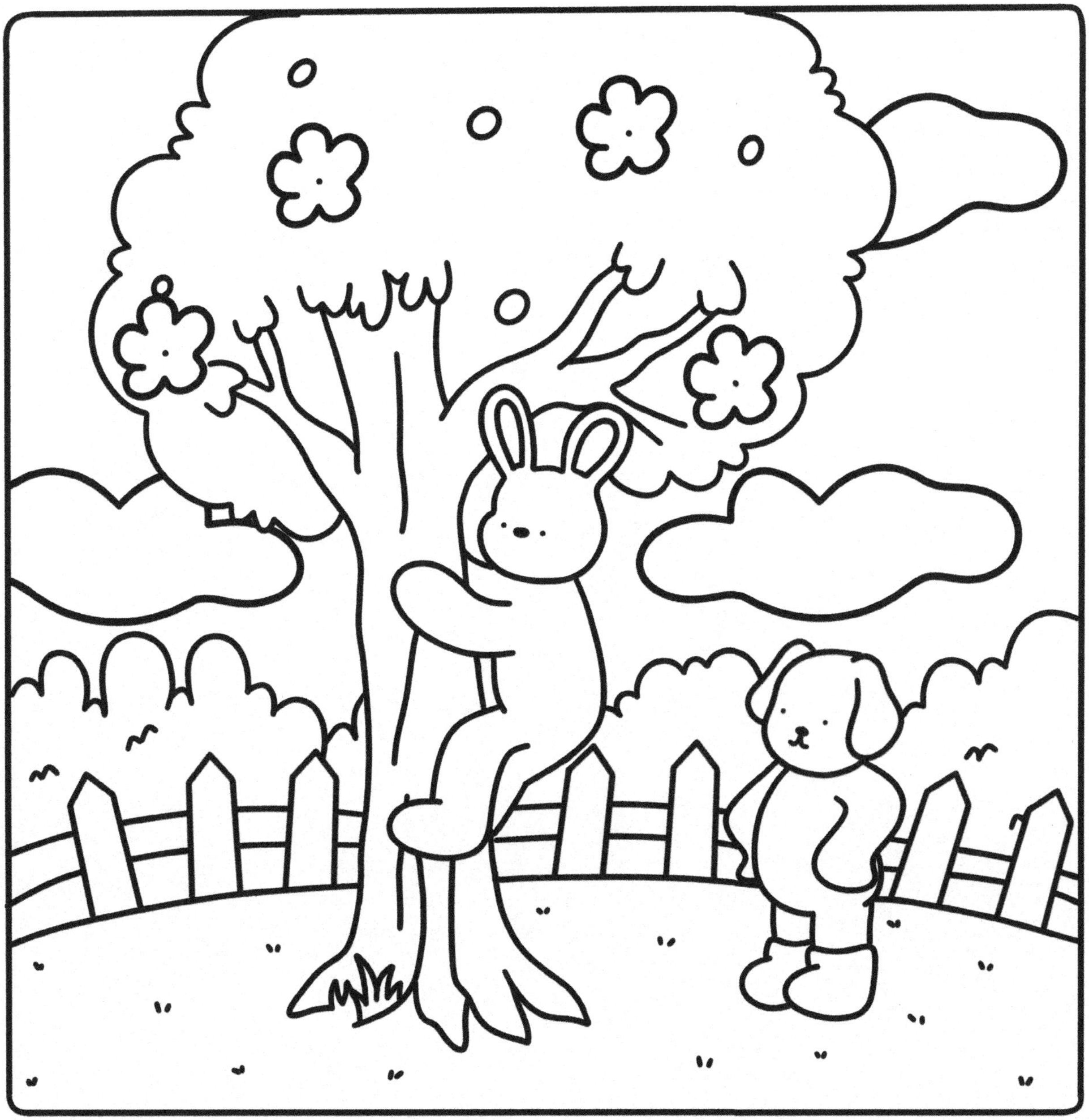

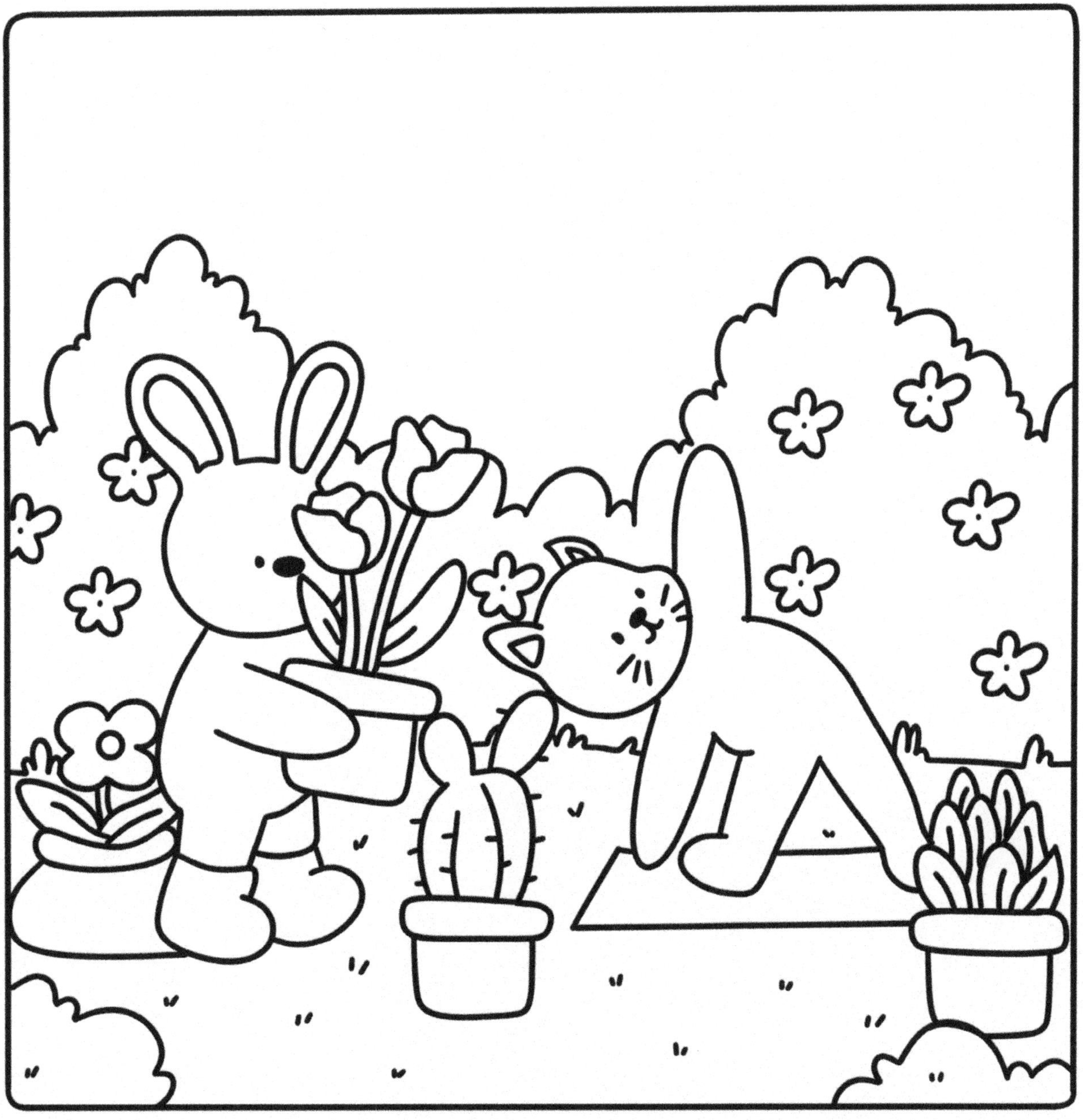

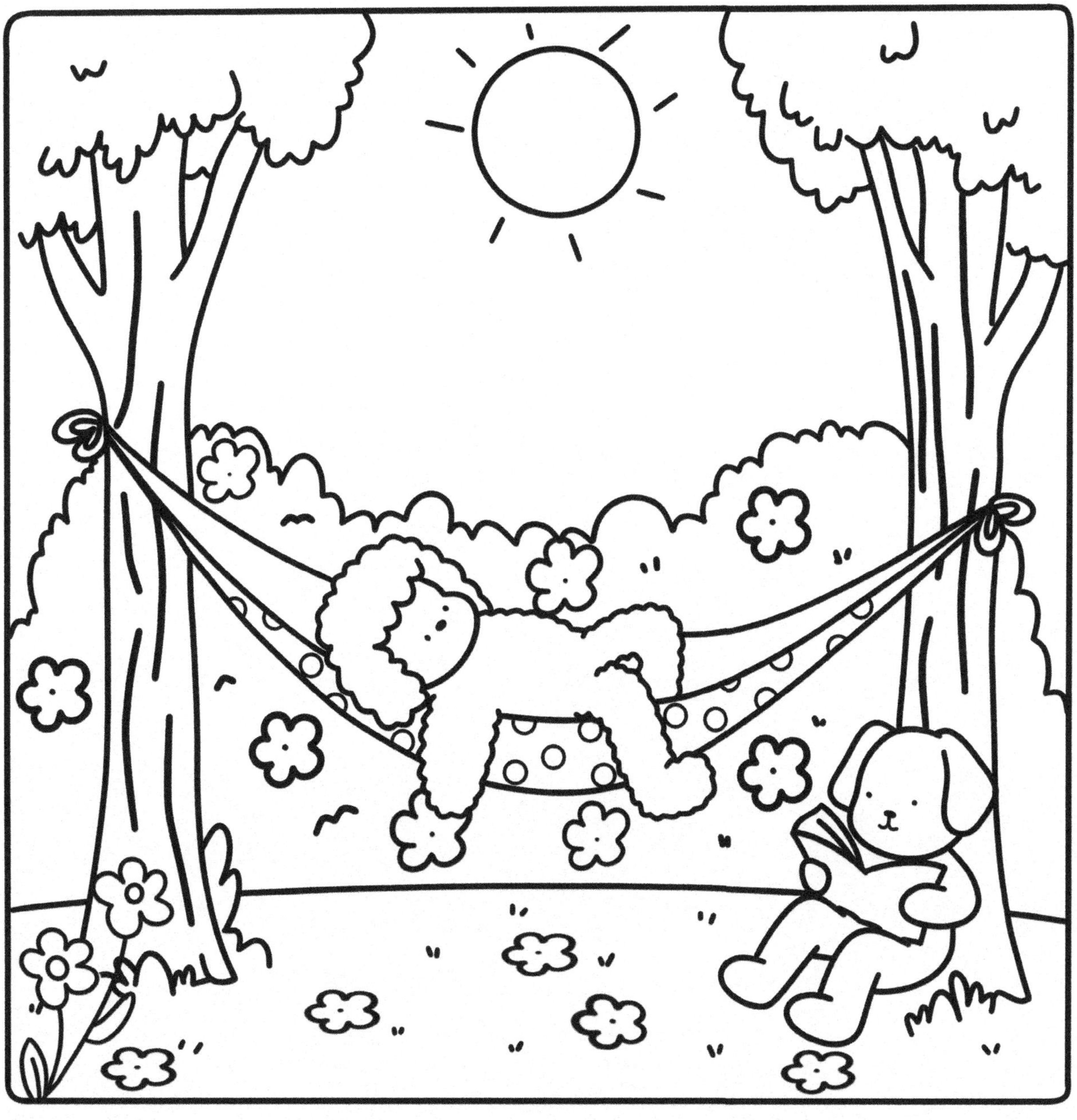

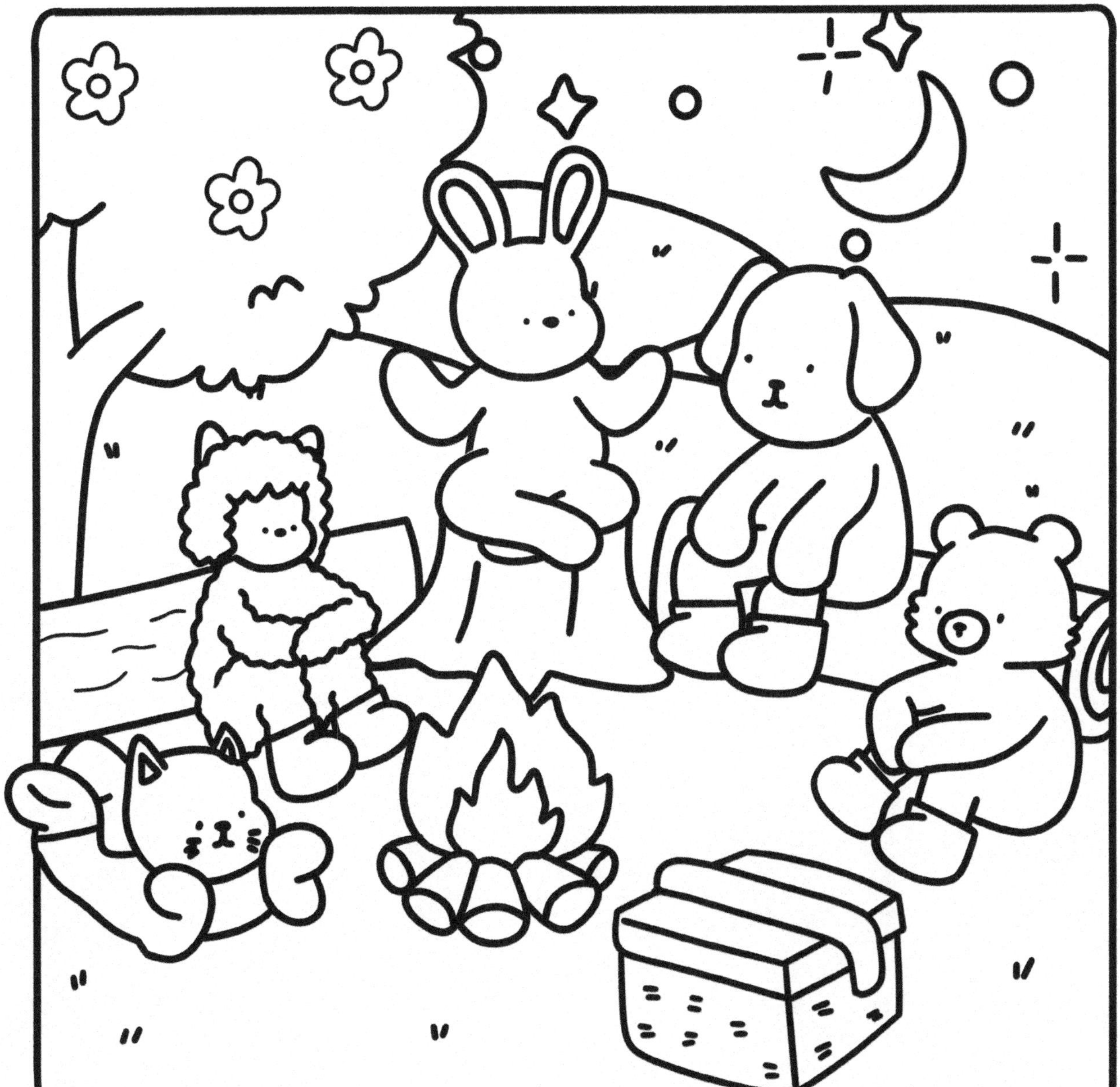

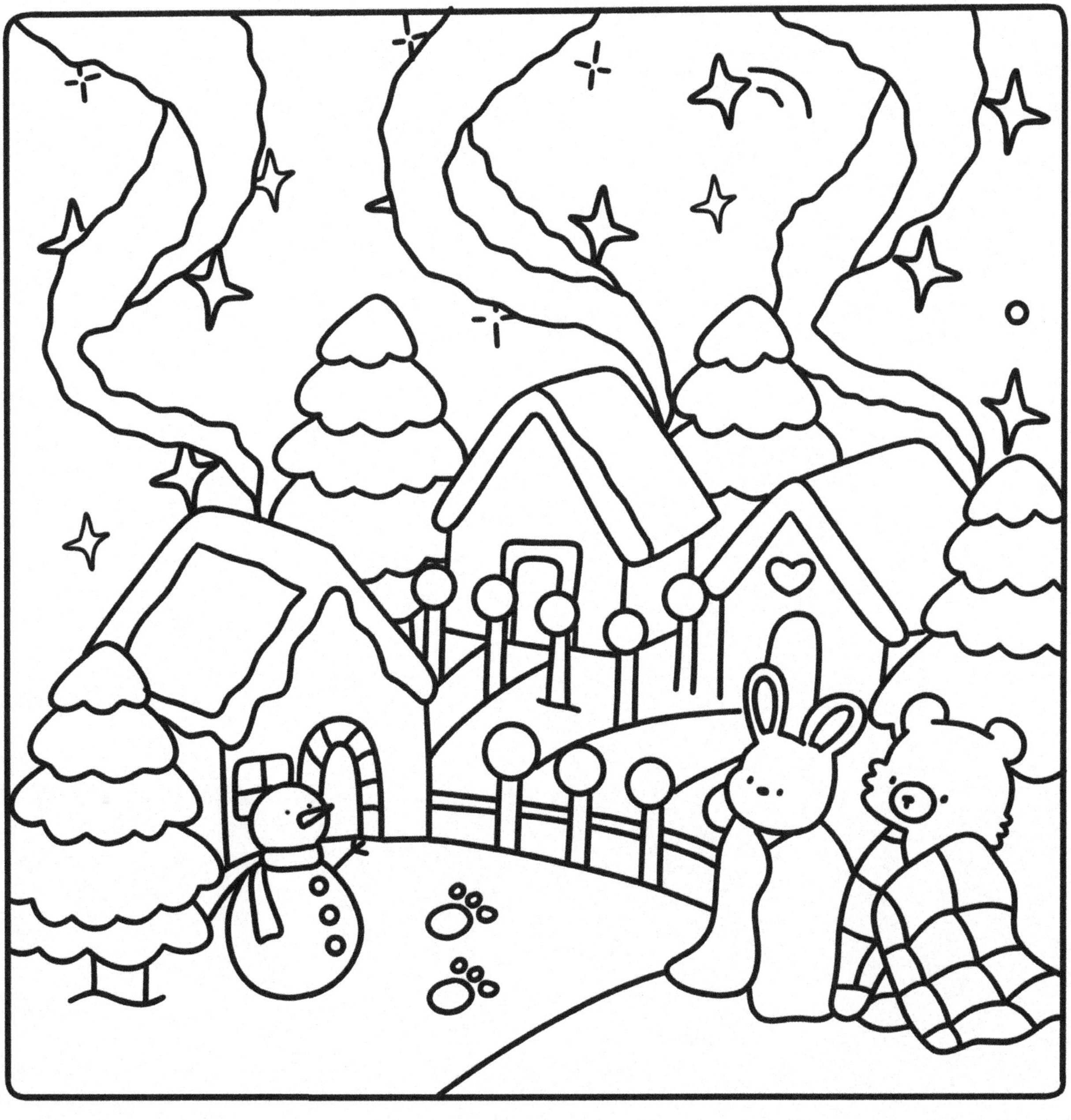

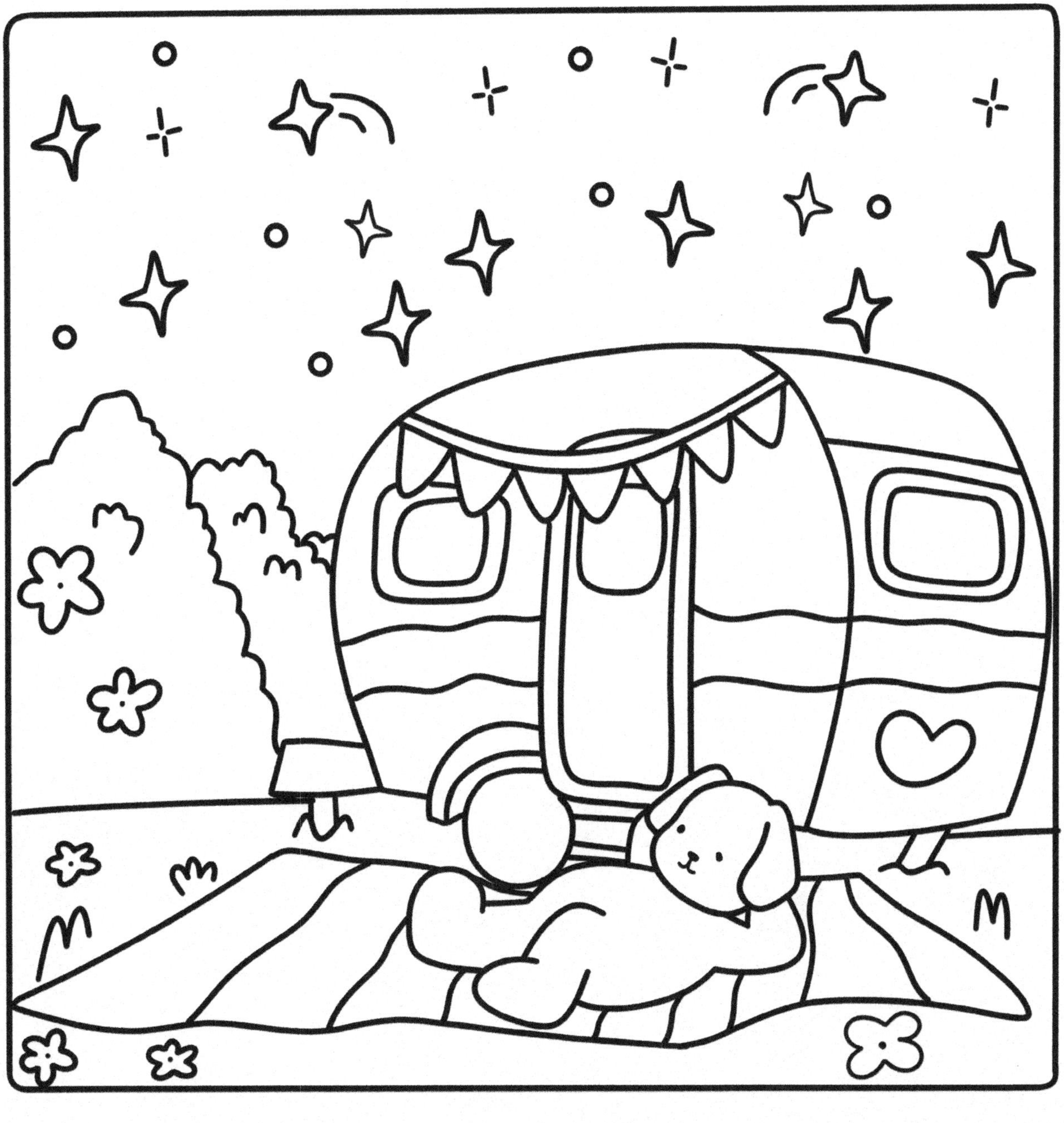

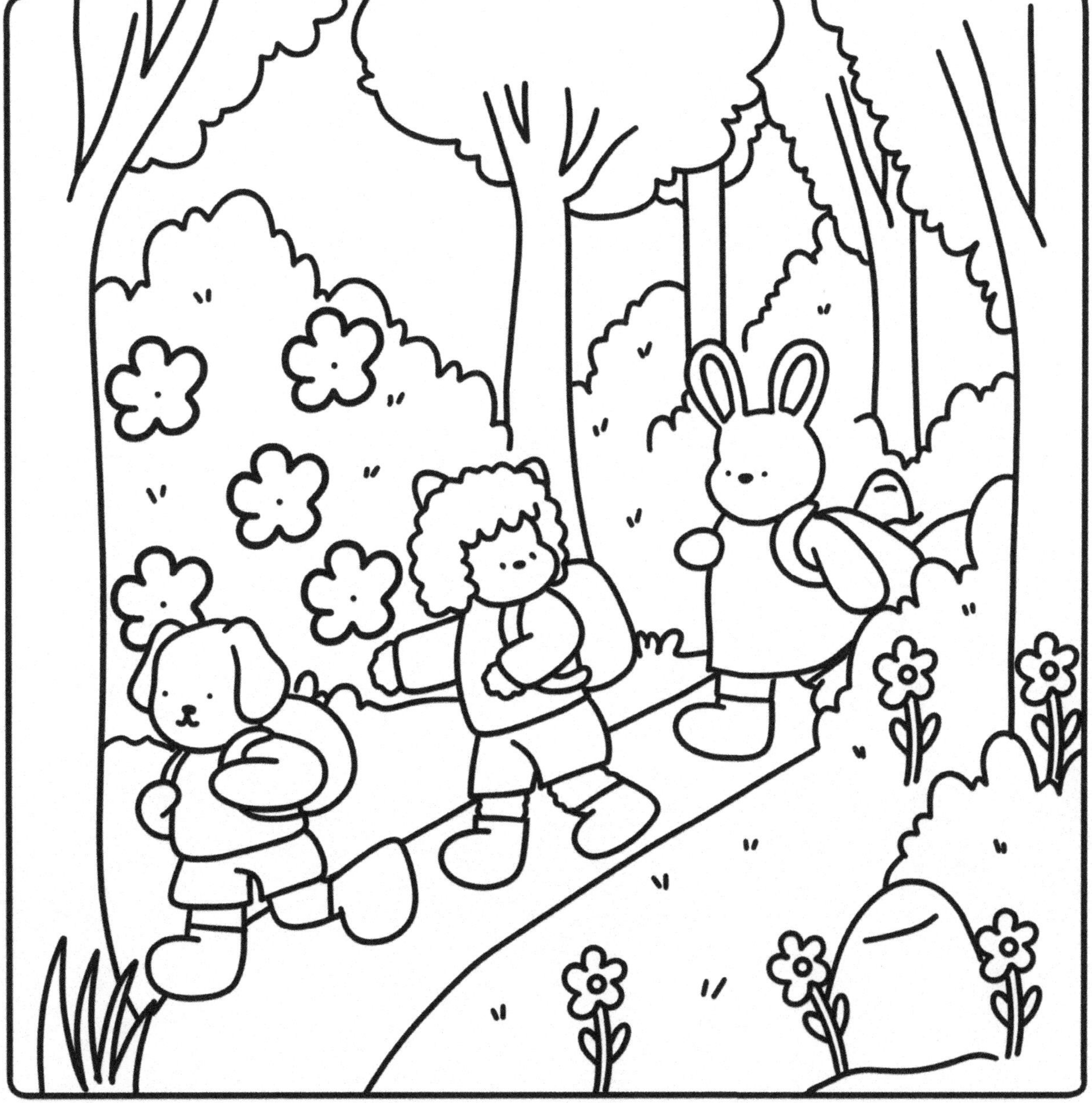

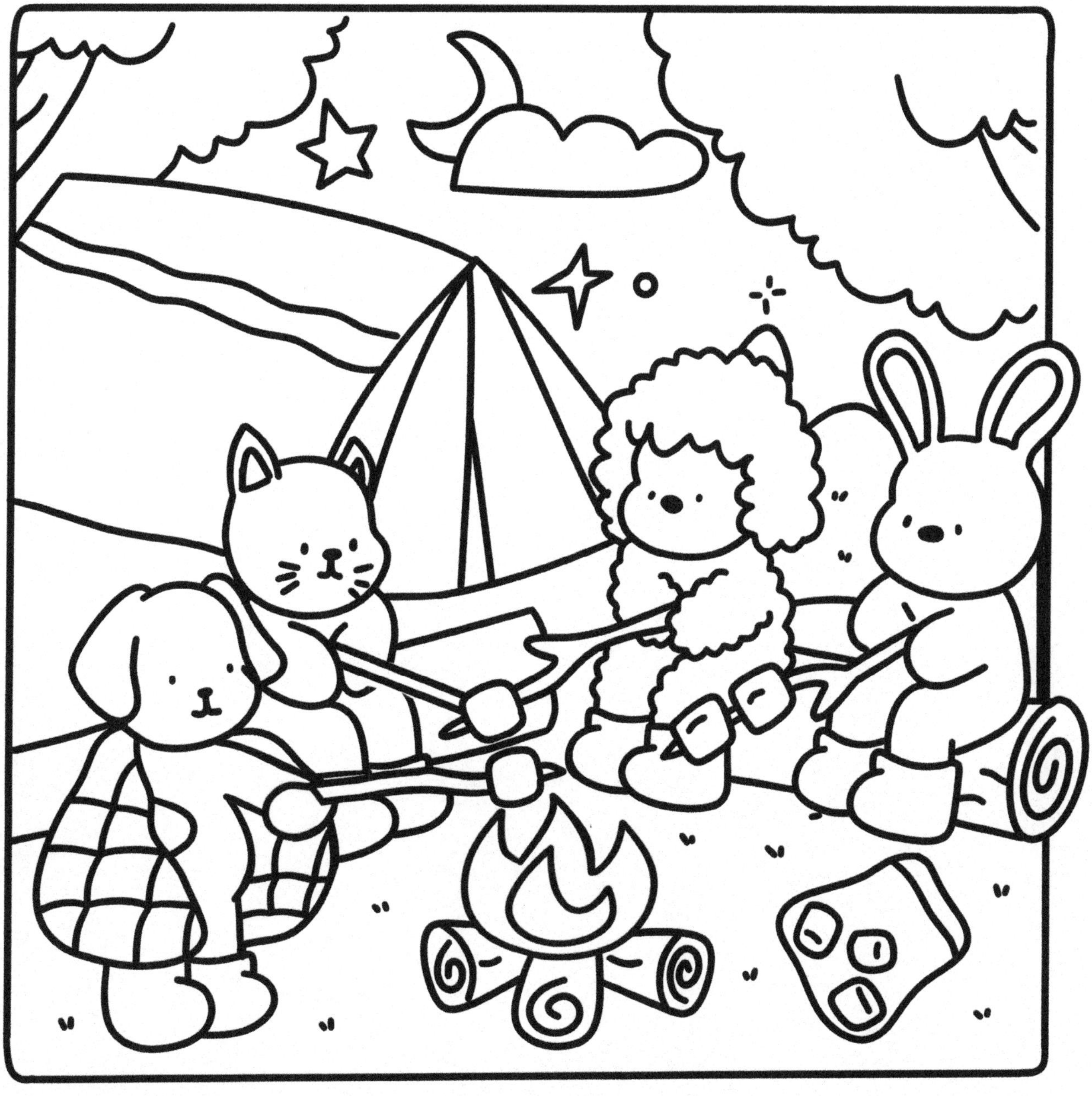

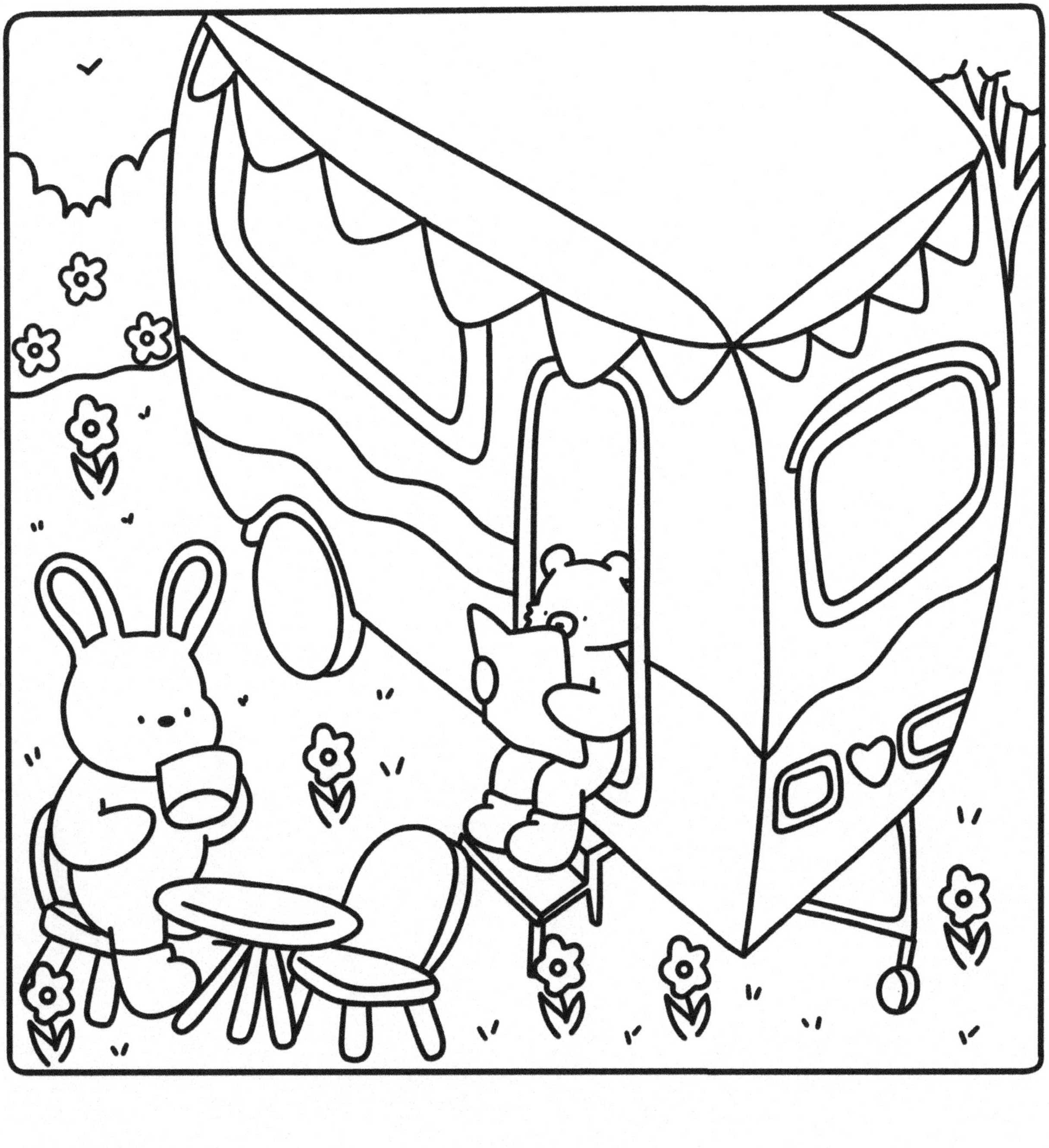

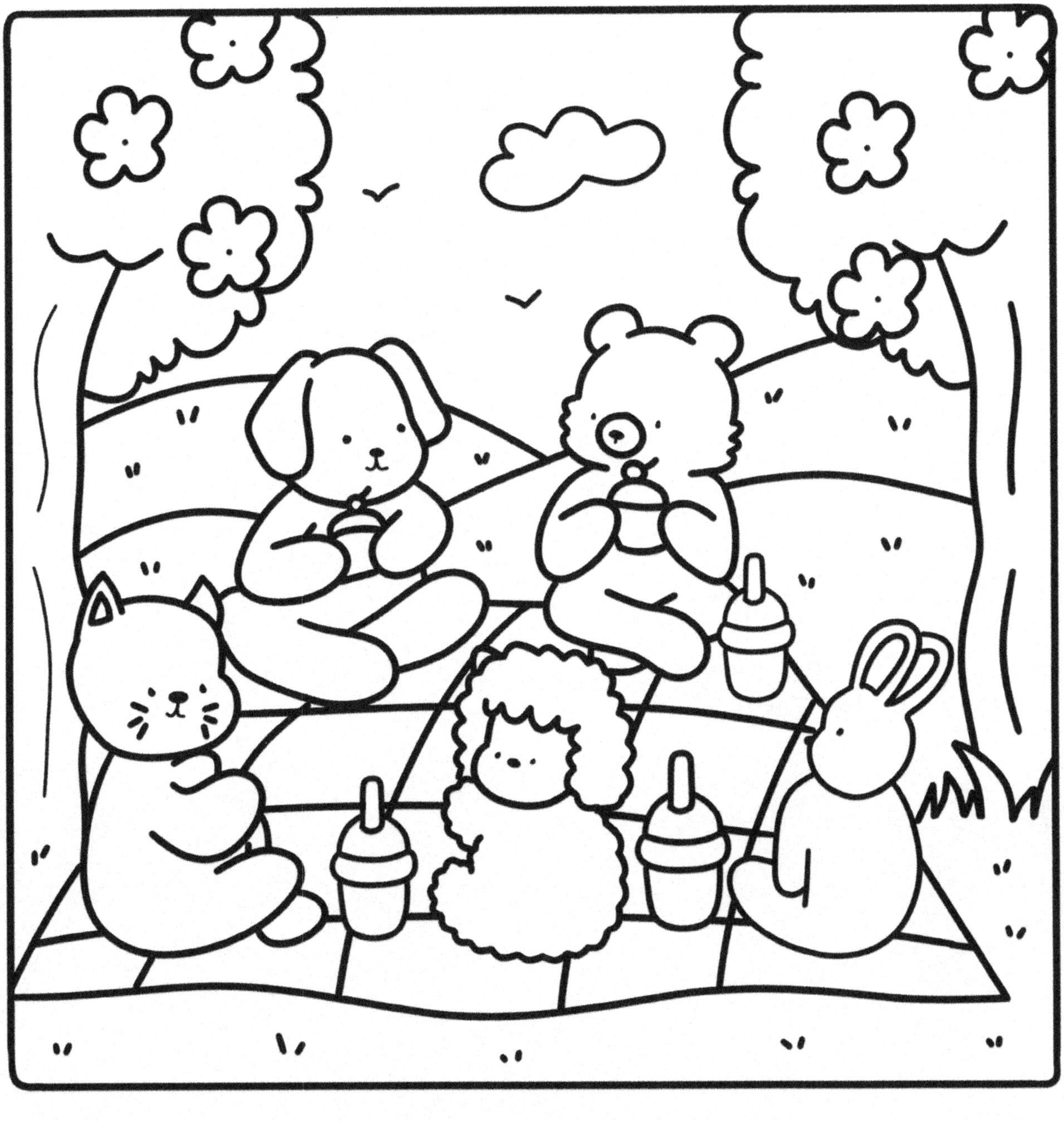

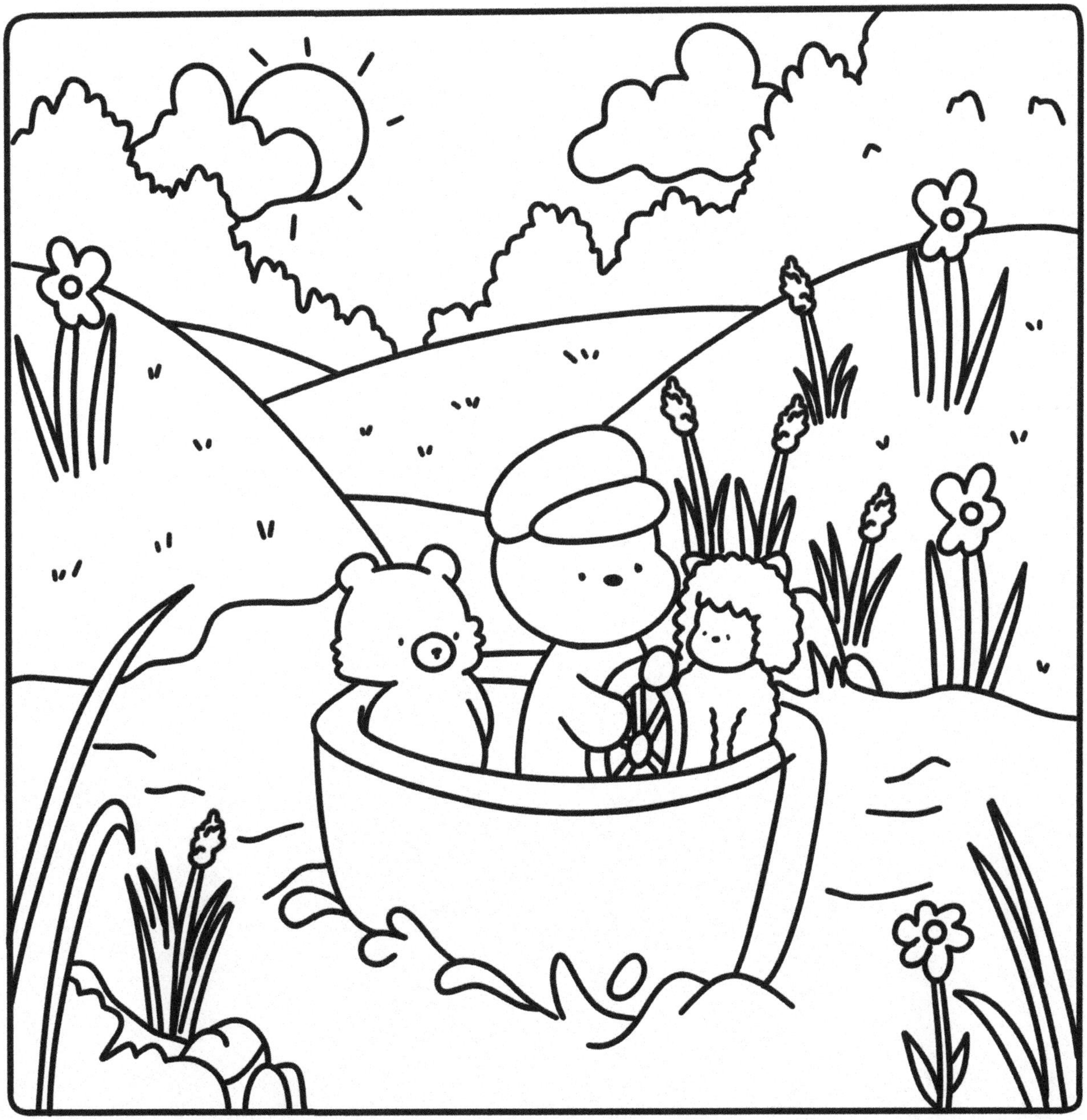

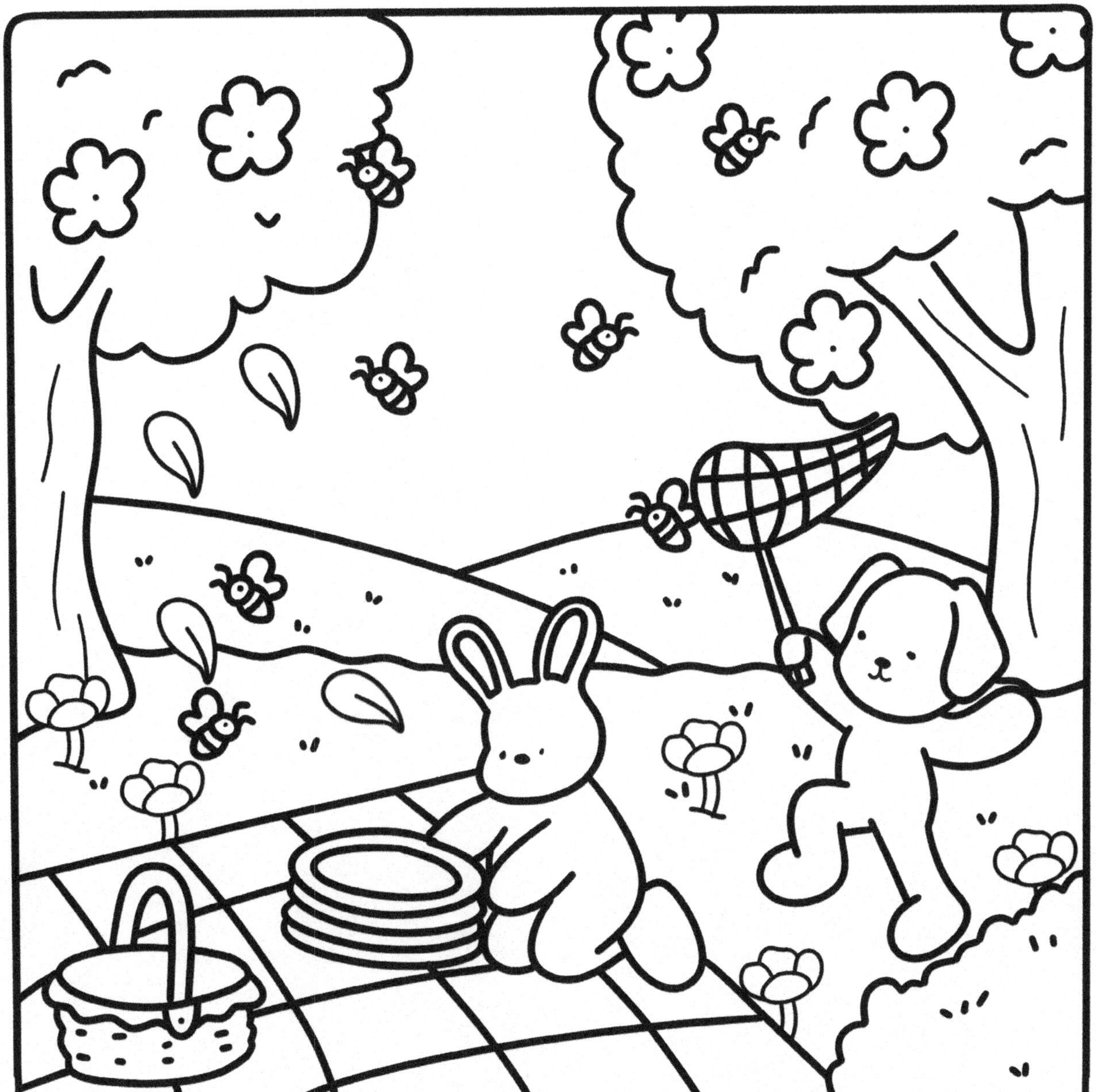

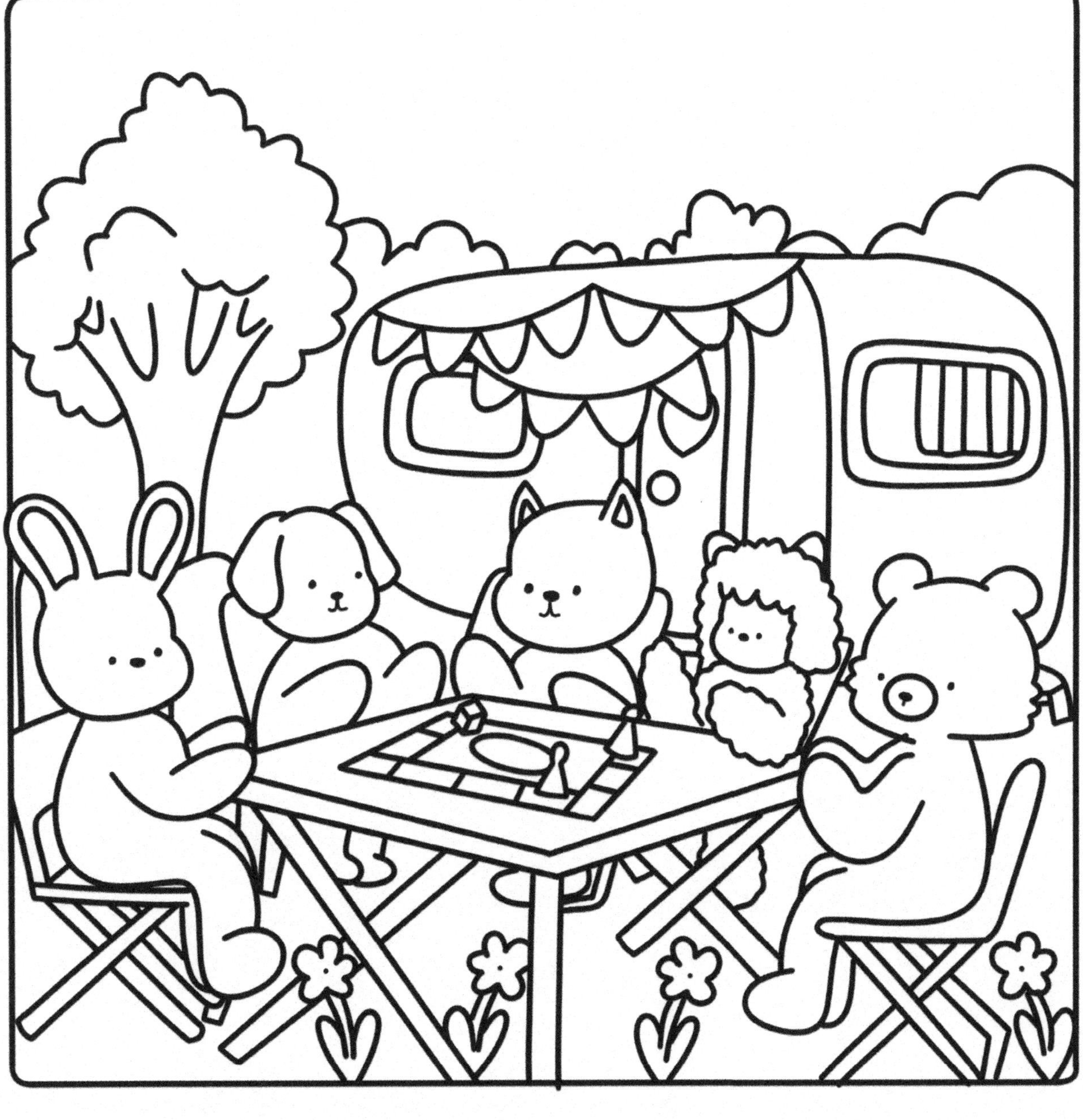

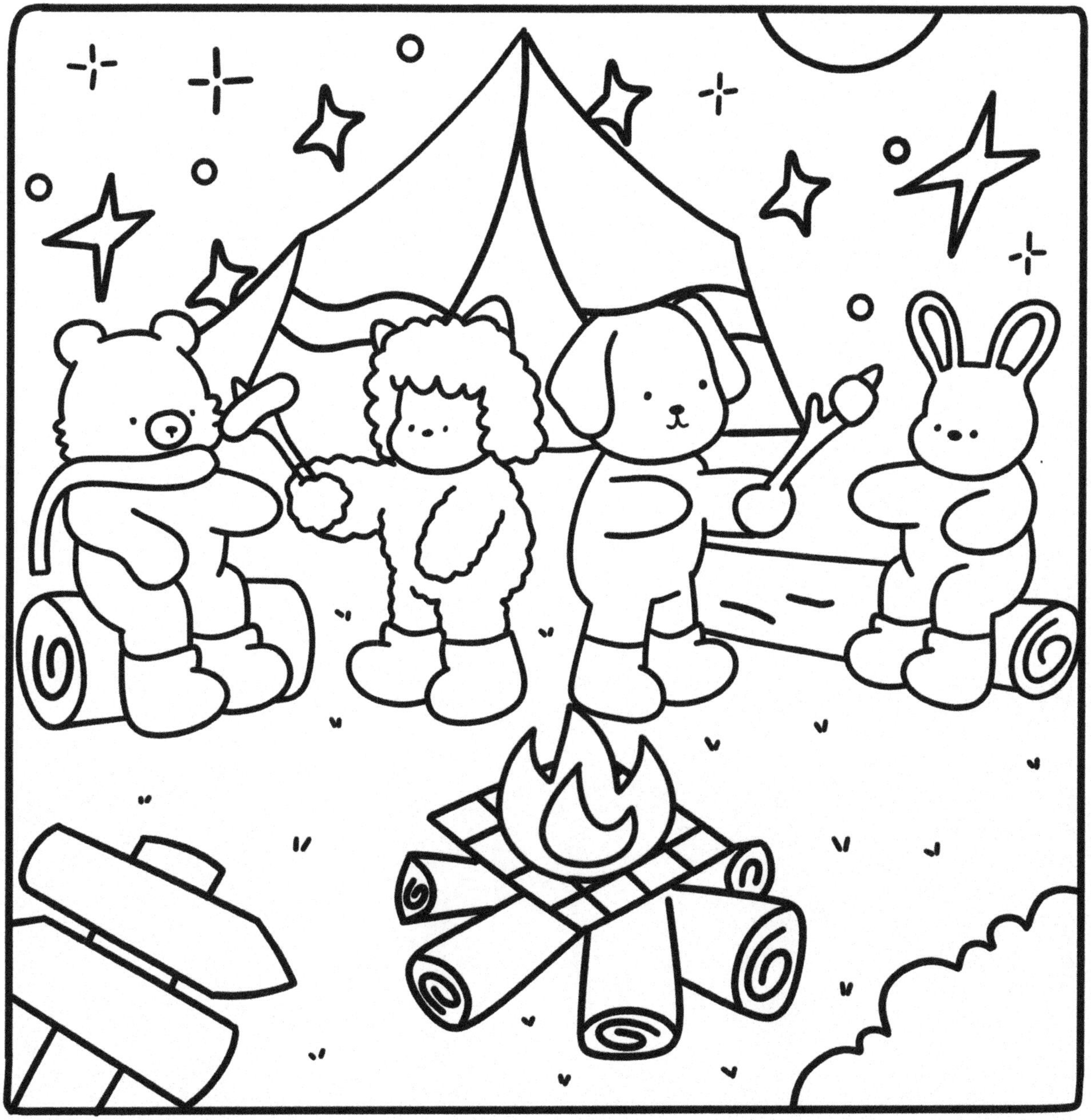

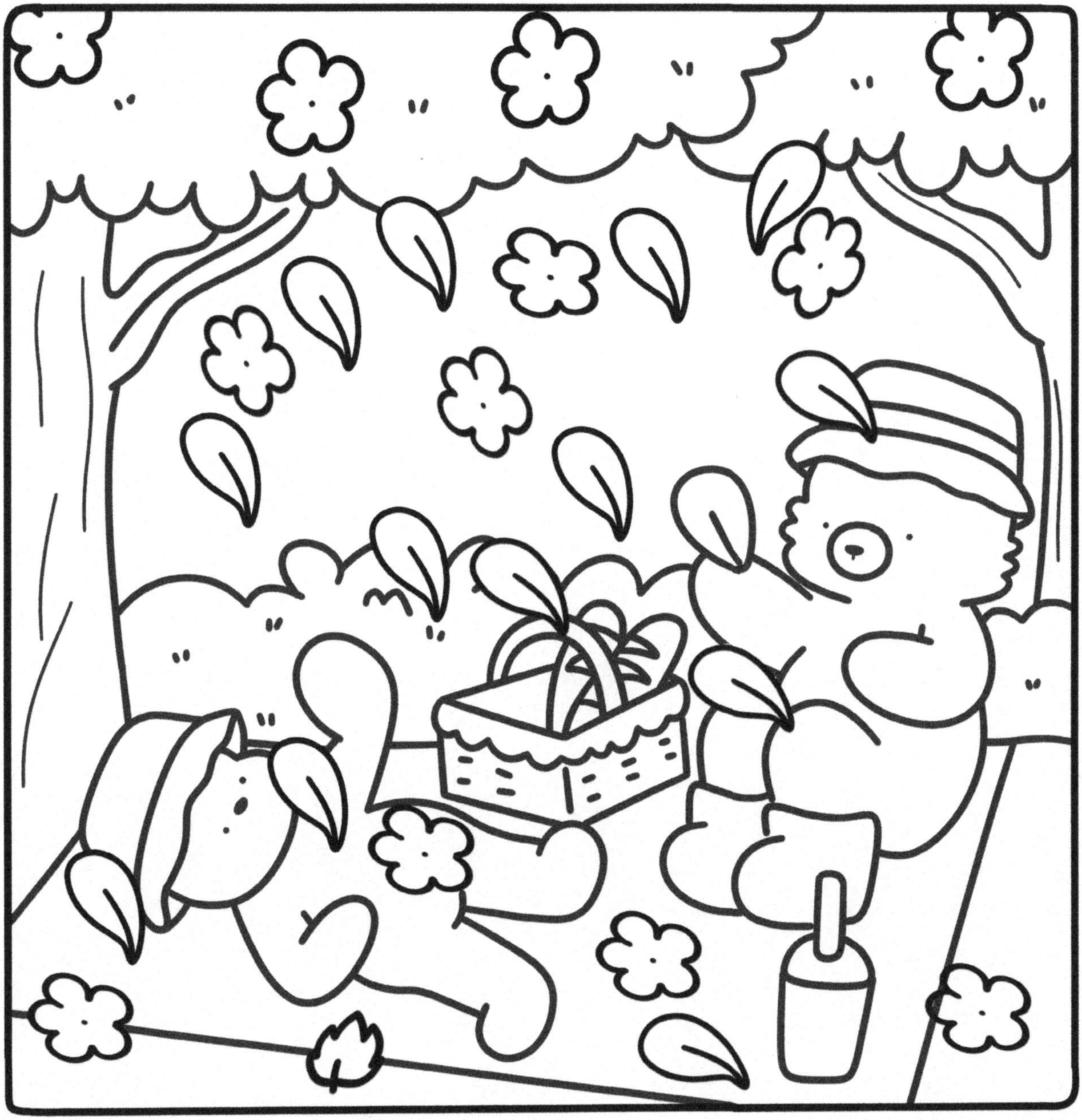

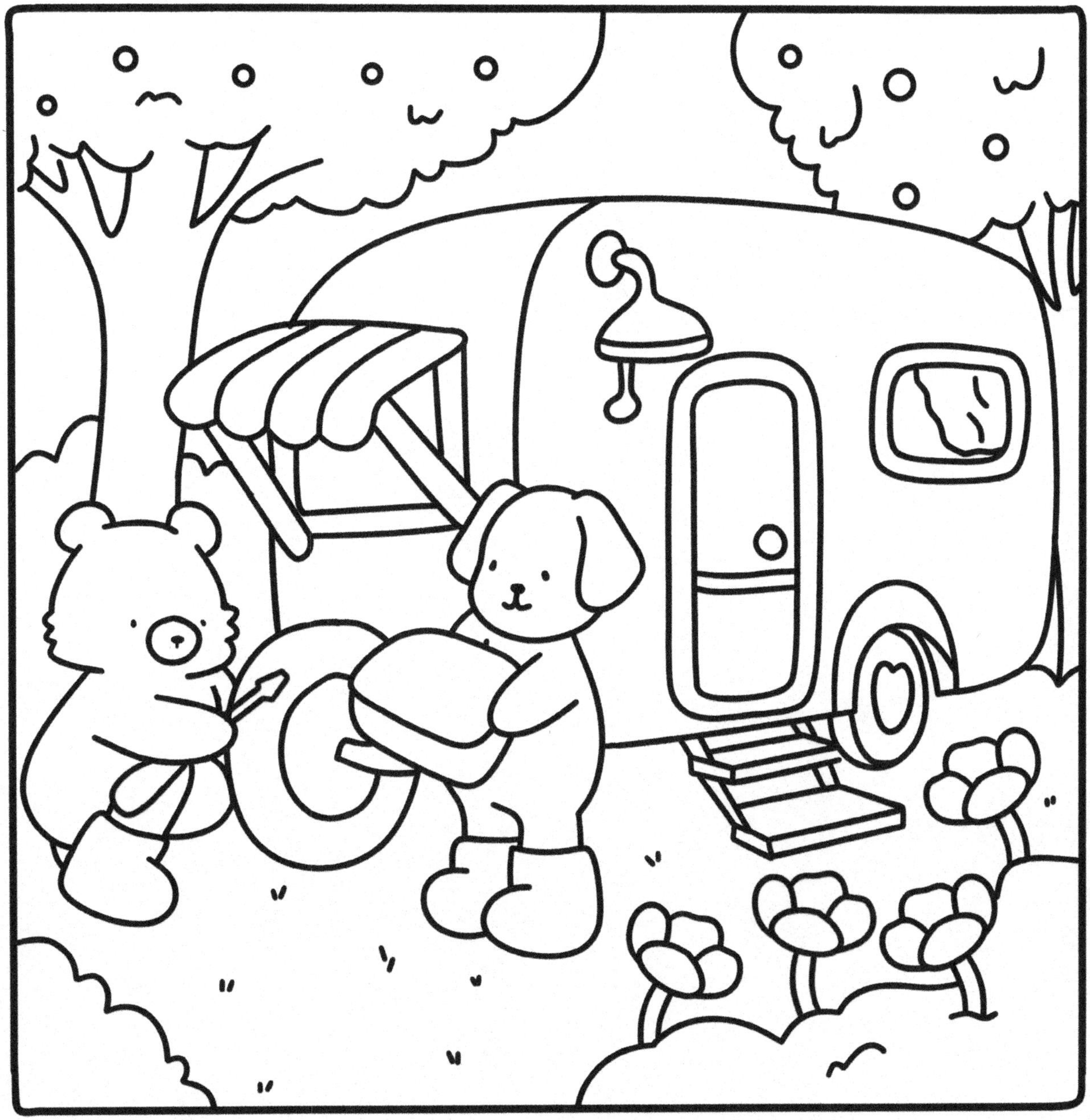

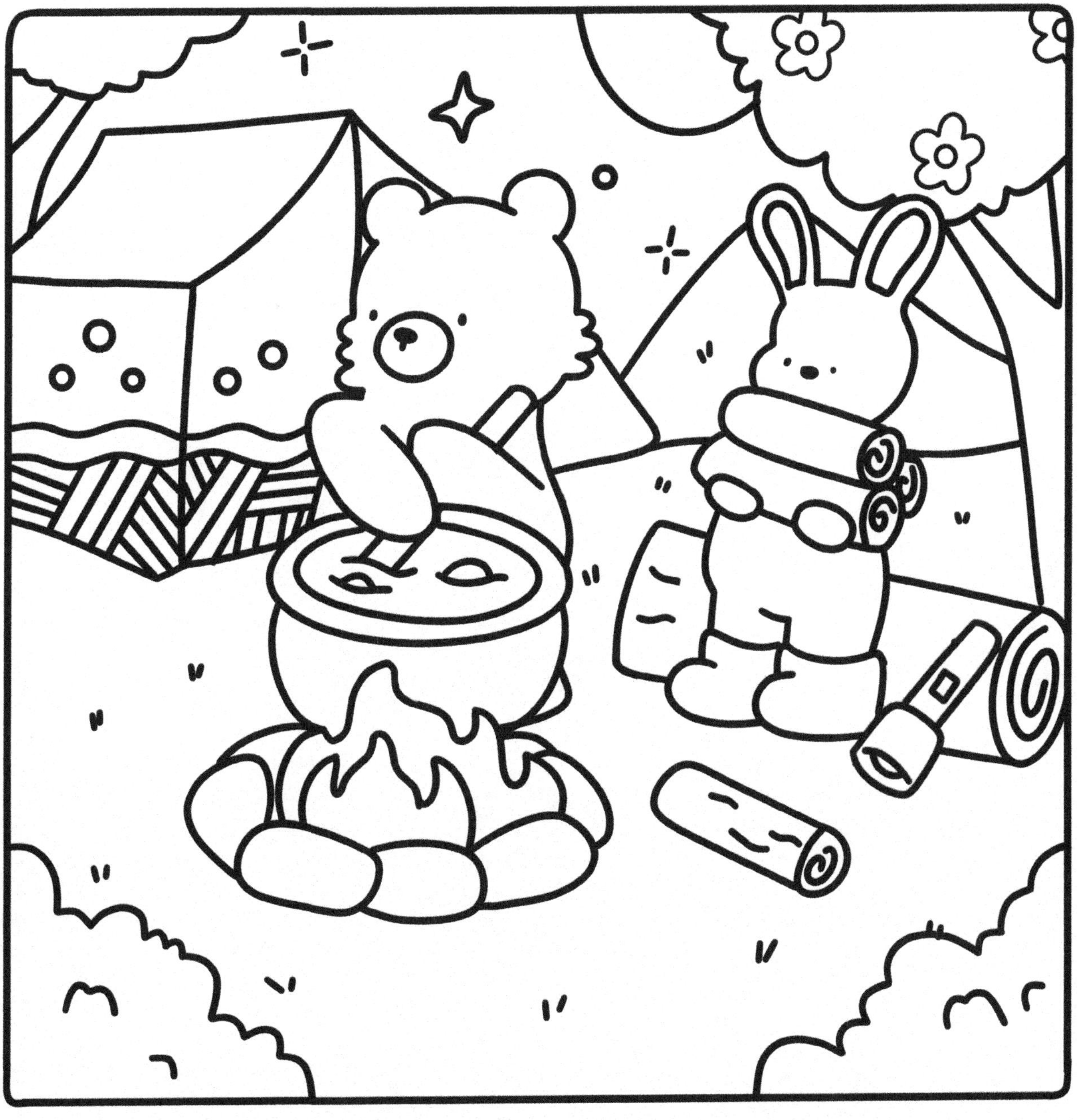

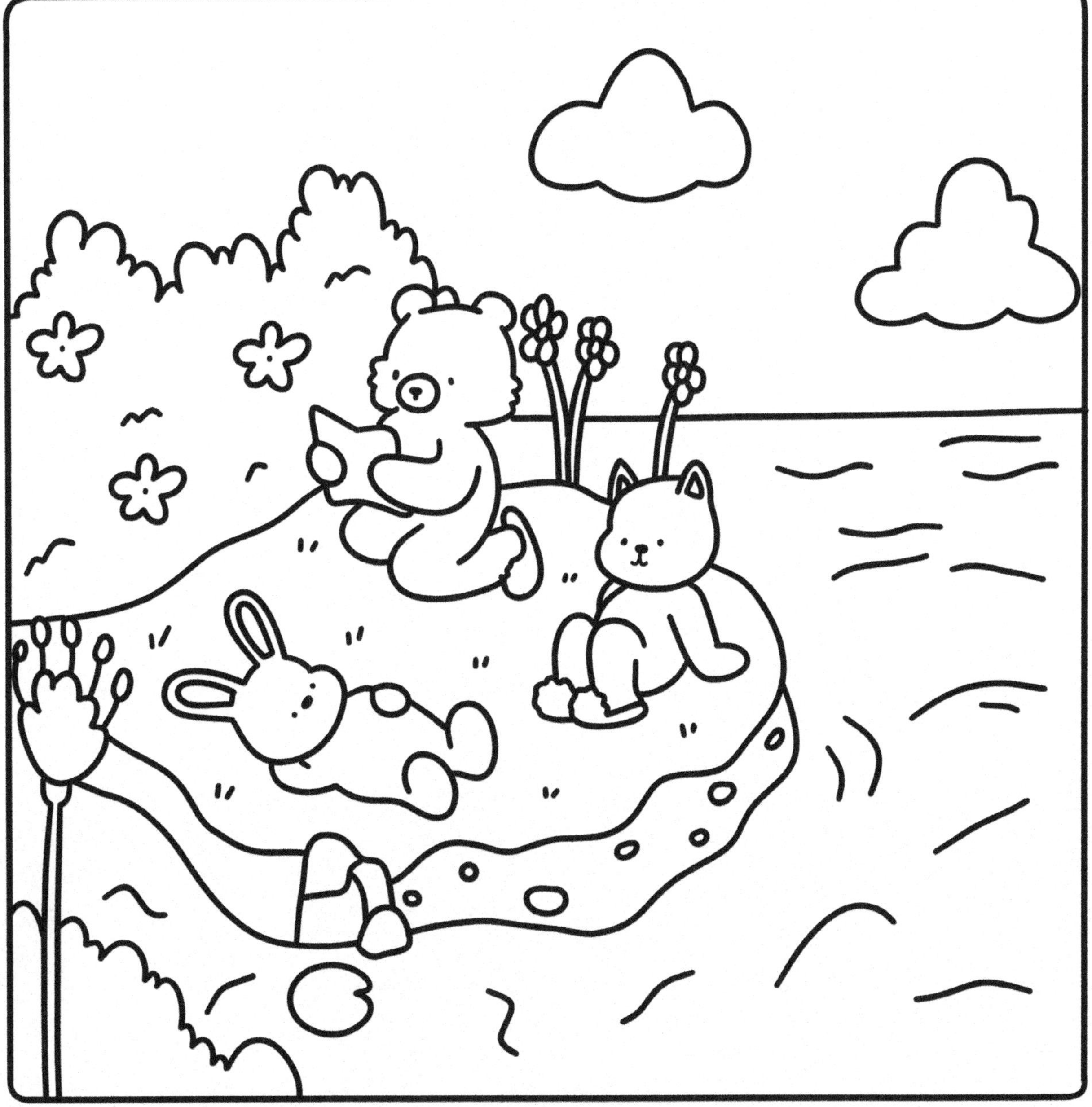

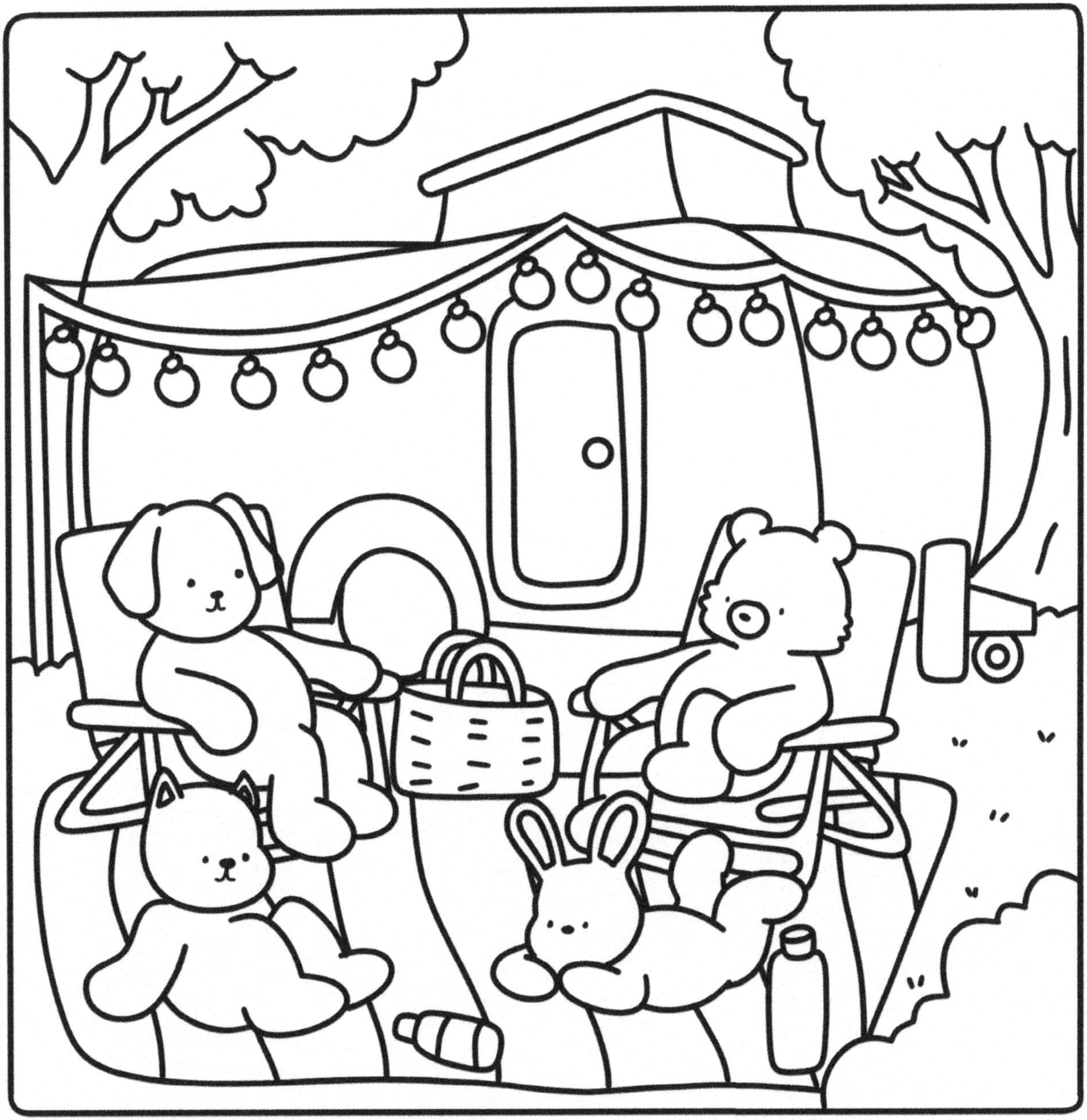

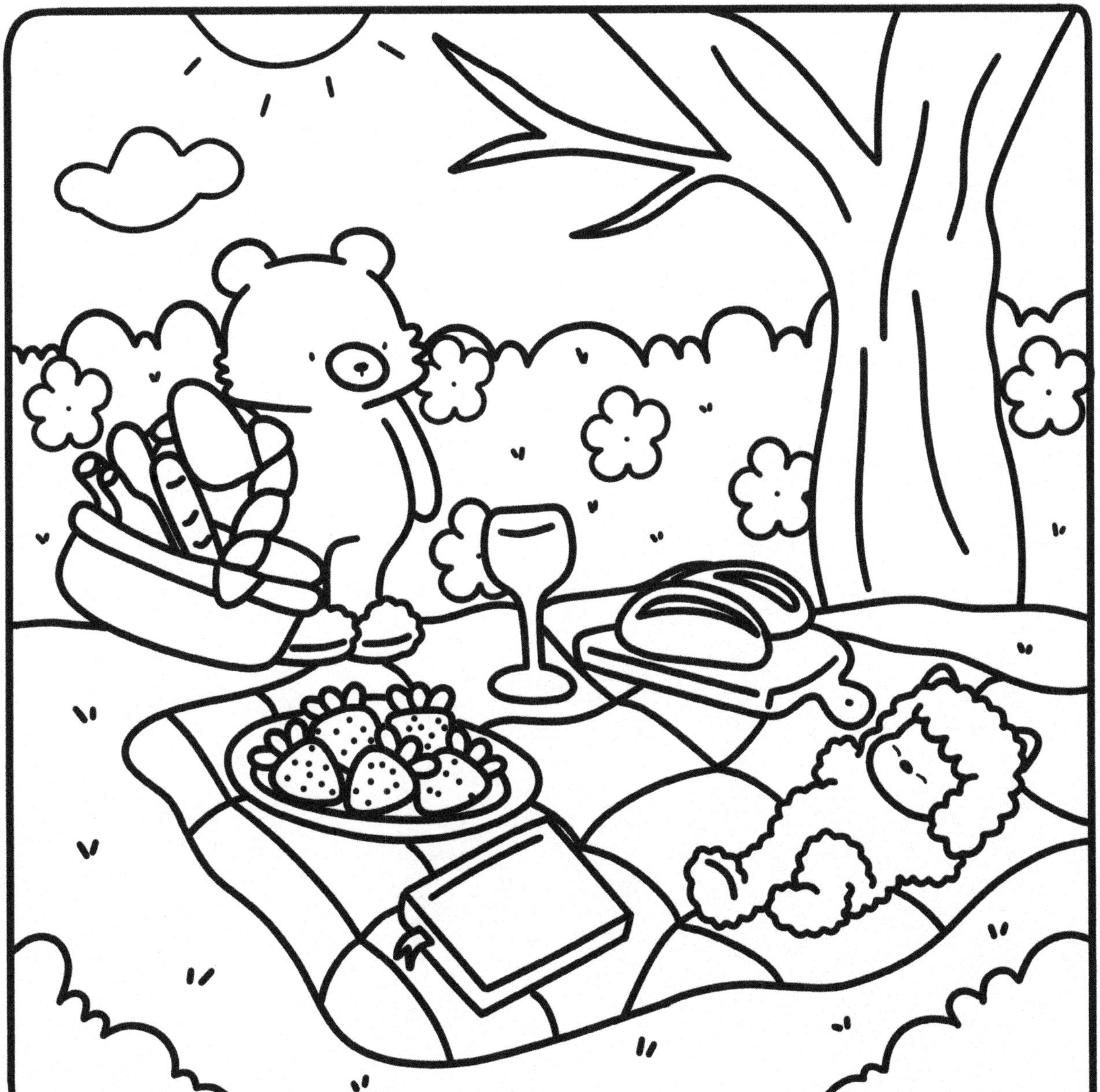

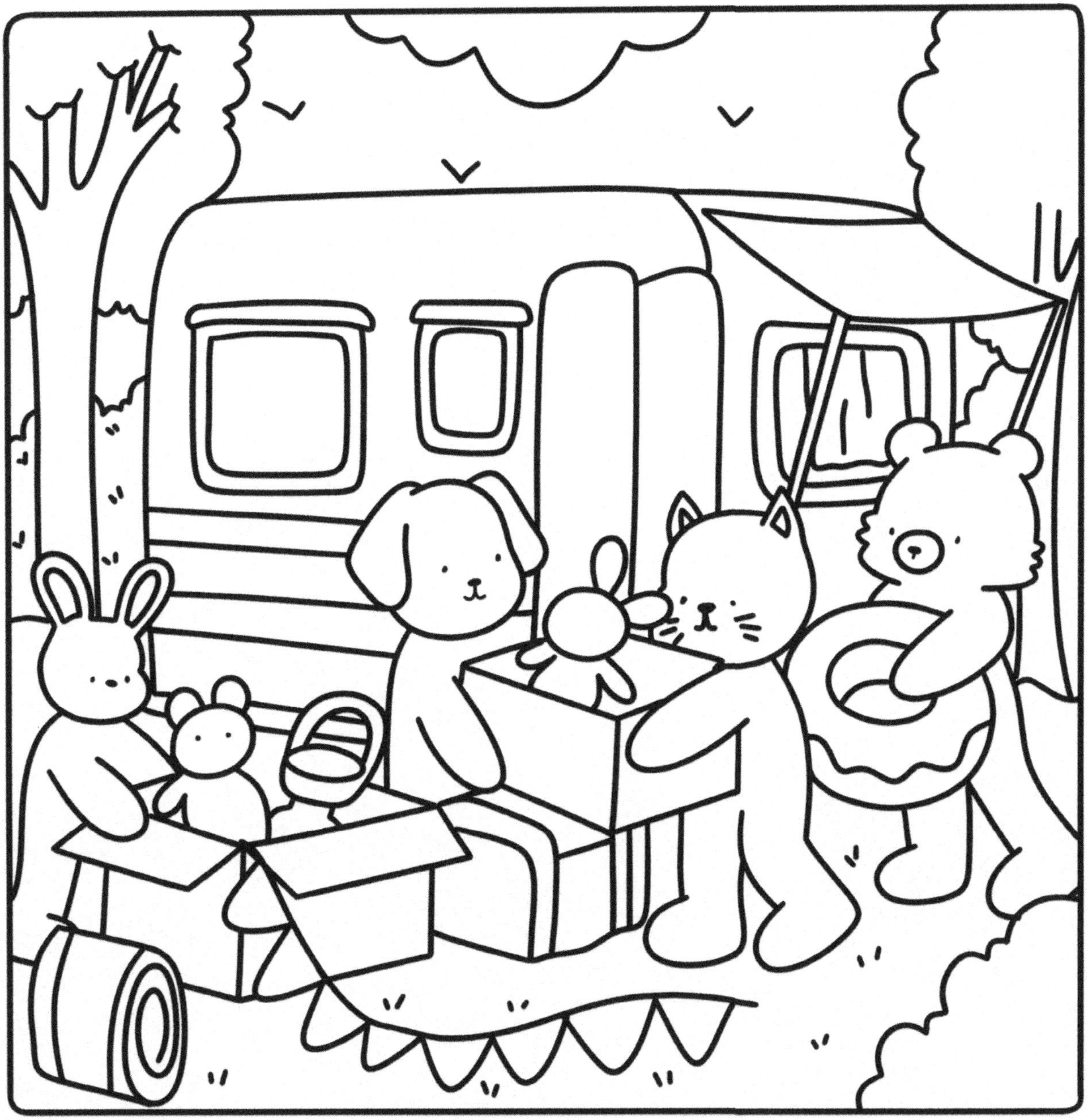

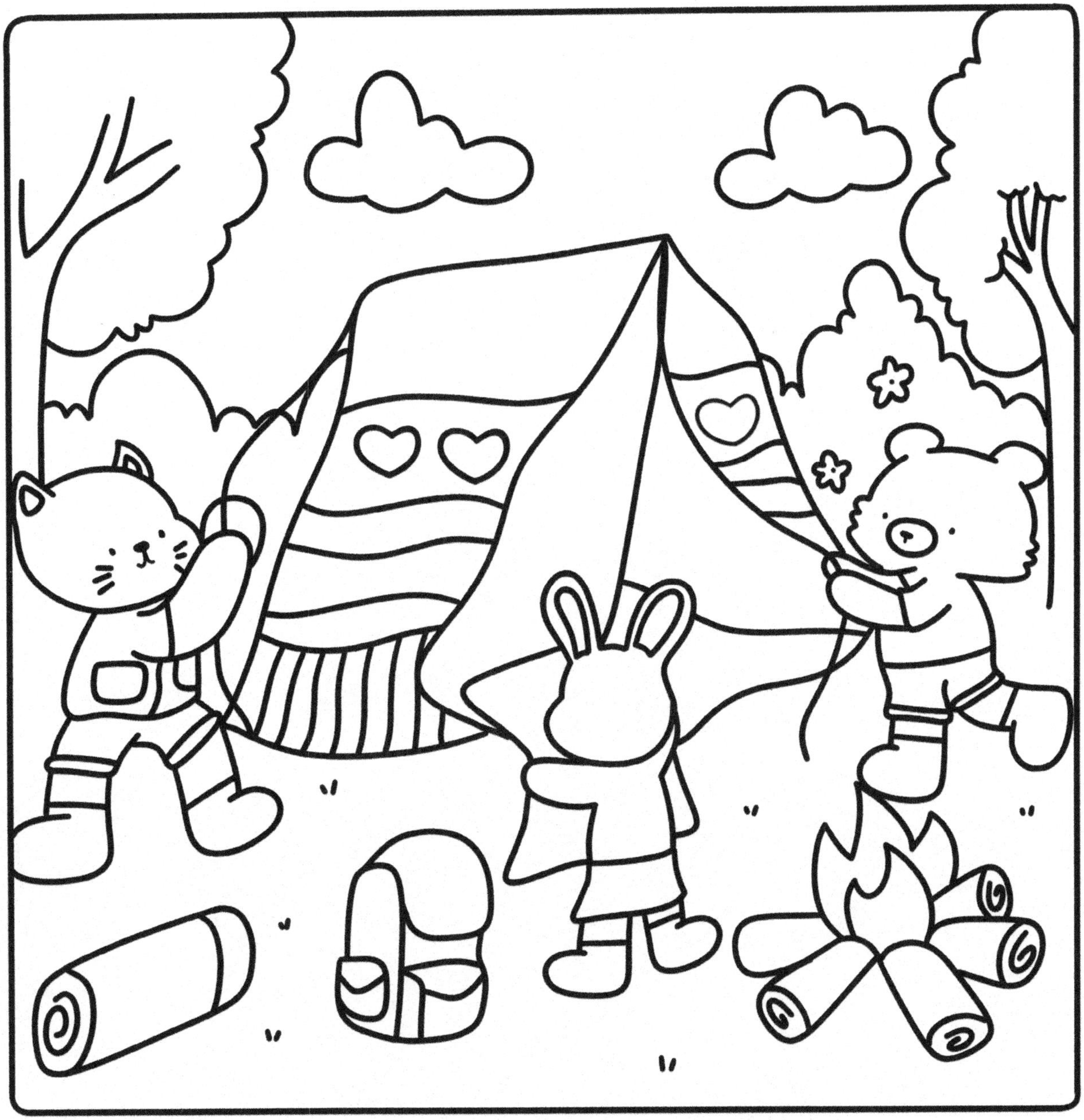

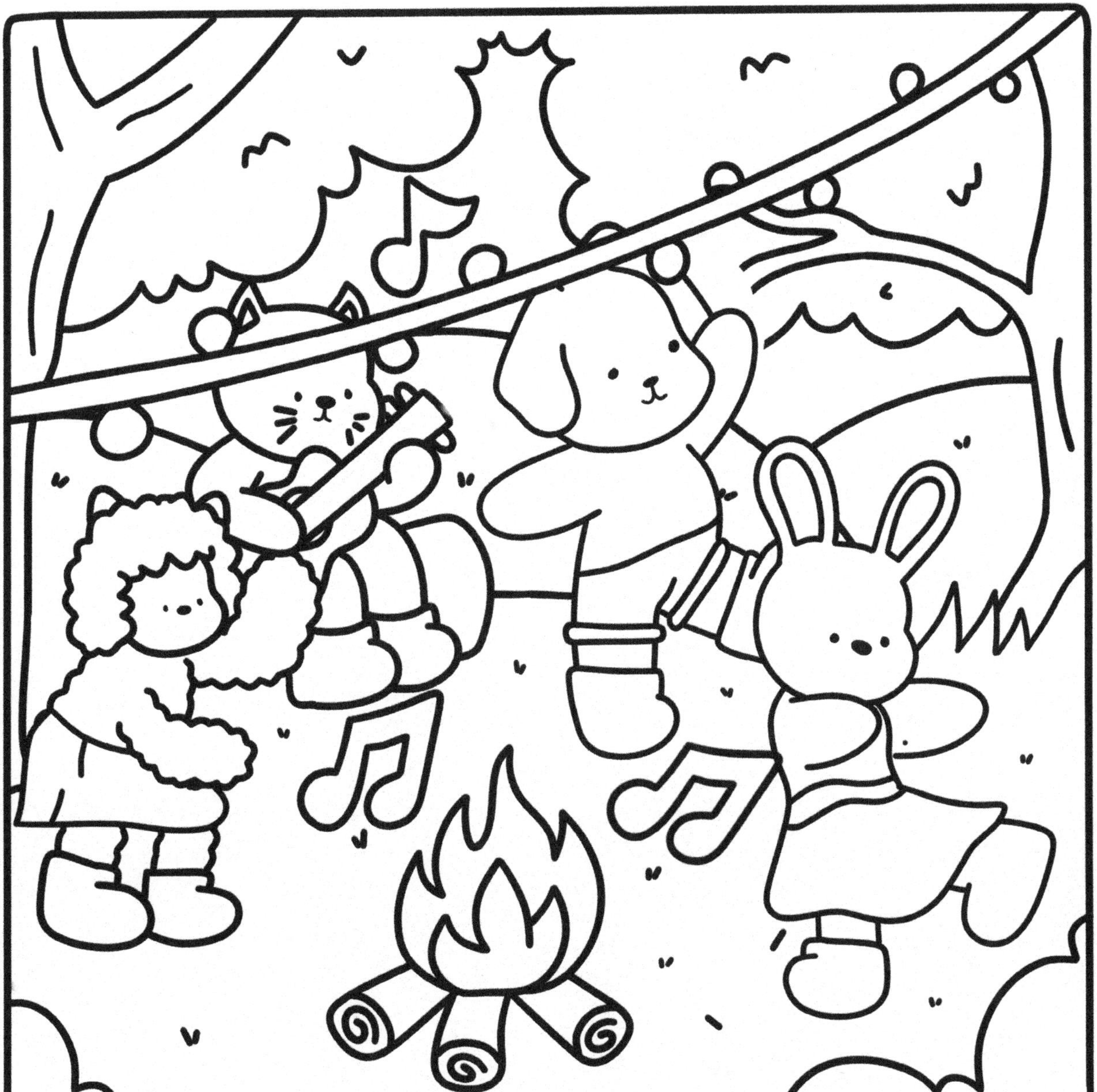

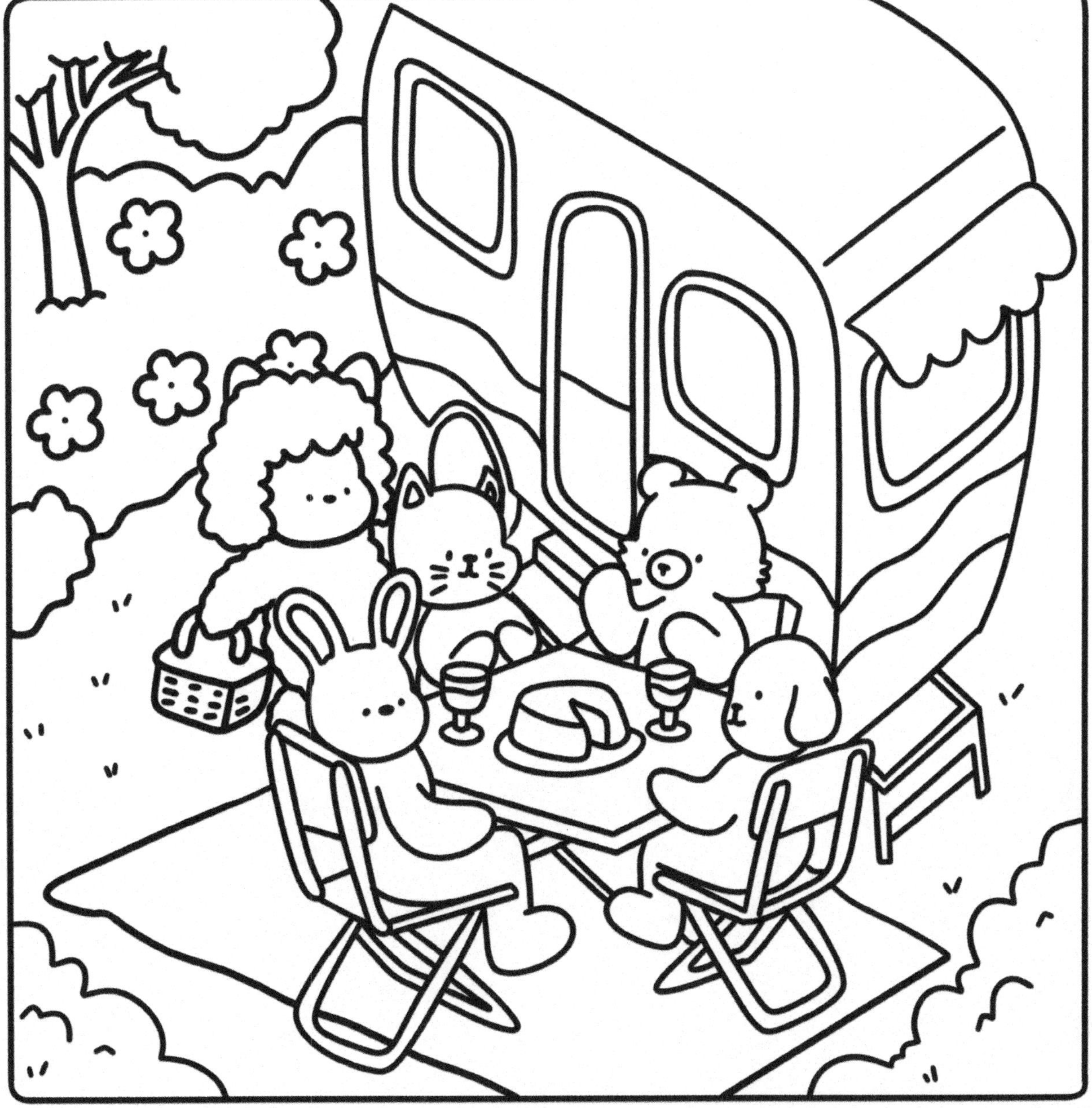

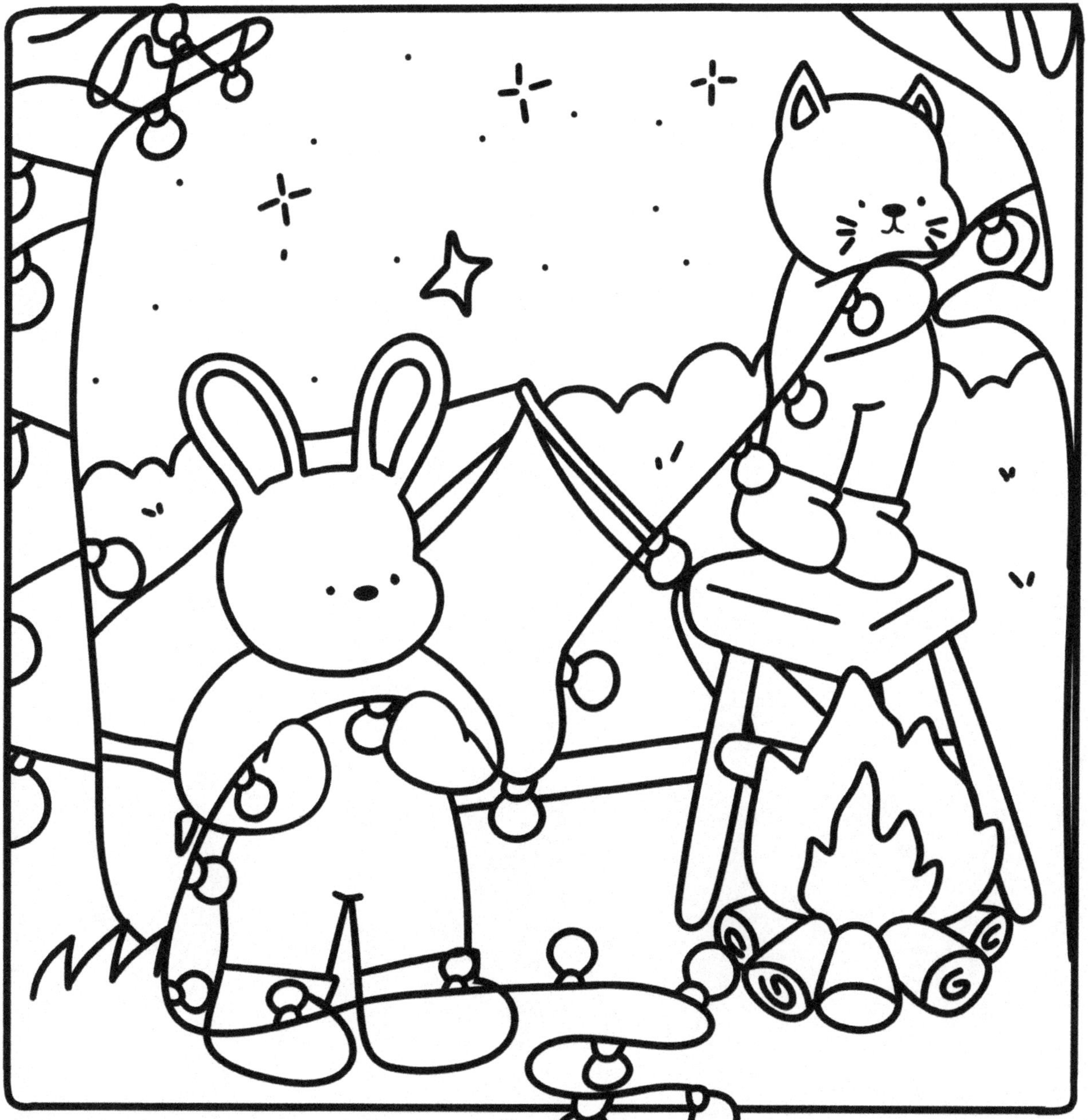

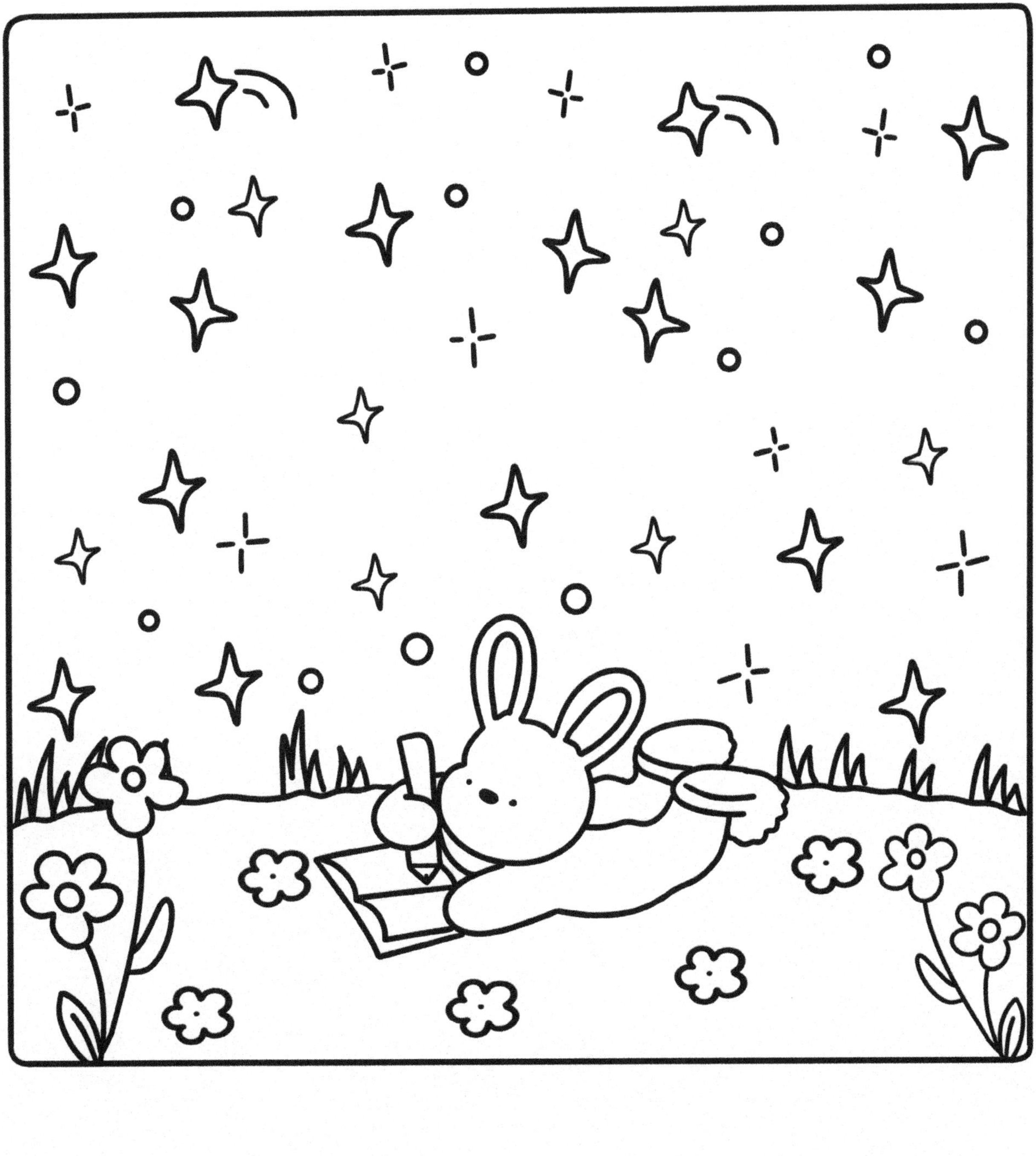

Made in the USA
Columbia, SC
13 July 2025